ALAN PATON SPEAKING

Books by Roy Holland

Insights and Outsights: Poems by Roy Holland
    Cape Town: David Philip. ISBN: 0864861214

Just A Bit Touched: Tales of Perspective
    Writers Club Press. ISBN: 0-595-15874-9

Flakes of Dark and Light: Tales from Southern Africa and Elsewhere
    Writers Club Press. ISBN: 0-595-17423-X

Pivot of Violence: Tales of the New South Africa
    Writers Club Press. ISBN: 0-595-15821-8

News From Parched Mountain: Tales from the Karoo in the new South Africa
    Writers Club Press. ISBN: 0-595-14612-0

The Waking & Making of Paul Gauguin – Conversations with Himself: A Play for Voices
    Diadem Books, 2008 ISBN: 978-0-9559741-3-7

Alan Paton Speaking: The Lintrose Conversations
    Edited by Charles Muller. Diadem Books, 2008.

The Jonathan Three (published by Diadem Books):

The Nowhere Man   ISBN: 978-0-9559741-0-6
Journey Towards Himself   ISBN: 978-0-9559741-1-3
Now Lead Me Home   ISBN: 978-0-9559741-2-0

ALAN PATON SPEAKING

THE LINTROSE CONVERSATIONS: INTERVIEW WITH ALAN PATON

Roy Holland

Edited by

Charles Muller

DIADEM BOOKS

All Rights Reserved. Copyright © 2008 Roy Holland & Charles Muller

No part of this book may be reproduced or transmitted in any form or by any means, graphic, electronic, or mechanical, including photocopying, recording, taping or by any information storage or retrieval system, without the permission in writing from the publisher.

Published by Diadem Books

For information, please contact:

Diadem Books
Ocean Surf
CLASHNESSIE
IV27 4JF
Scotland UK

www.diadembooks.com

Book and cover design by Angus Muller

ISBN: 978-0-9559741-4-4

ACKNOWLEDGEMENTS

Grateful thanks are due to Sony without whose kind assistance the interview in this book would have been lost. The original tape recordings of the interview with Alan Paton, after some years, seemed to have become stuck together and would not play. When Roy Holland sent them to Japan, Sony fixed them and completely re-recorded a new set of tapes for him, at no cost, just in the interest of research. I commend Sony for this kind service, which enabled the typist, my daughter Valerie Kotkin-Smith, to transcribe the tapes in the first place.

Both of us, Roy and I, are of course grateful to Valerie Kotkin-Smith for her patience and meticulous care in typing the interview from the recordings. We appreciate that the job was an arduous one, listening to the tapes and winding them back again and again in order to get everything just right.

My sincere thanks are also due to my son Angus Muller for his invaluable expertise in the technical design of the book and cover.

A copy of the actual tape recording of the interview is obtainable on CD for a fee. Please contact me at Diadem Books, or by email publish@diadembooks.co.uk

Charles Muller
Editor
www.diadembooks.com

Table of Contents

INTRODUCTION 1

THE LINTROSE CONVERSATIONS 15

FICTION AND HISTORY: 87
Fact and Invention in Alan Paton's novel
Cry, the Beloved Country

INTRODUCTION

Alan Paton was born in 1903 and died in 1988. He is one of the most famous writers and political activists that South Africa has produced. He was deprived of his passport in 1960 when he came back from a Conference in Geneva, Switzerland; his passport was restored to him in 1970.

The first time I met him was in April 1970. At that time, I was Senior Lecturer in English at the University of Botswana, Lesotho and Swaziland (UBLS), which served the three African countries named, and whose main Campus was at Roma, twenty miles from the capital of Maseru in Lesotho. I wrote to him when he was living in Kloof, Natal, South Africa, and asked if I could come to see him as I was working on a thesis, registered with the University of Sussex, in England. He said 'Yes' and I duly visited him there for an initial meeting. Nothing was recorded at this meeting; it was really an opportunity for me to introduce myself, and for him 'to weigh me up', and generally to converse. He was careful to sound out what political affiliations I might have had. As it happened, I had none, although my sympathies were clear. (He was harassed by the South African Special Police, and possibly other 'rightist' groups.) It was, of course, after the notoriety he had gained during his years at Diepkloof Boys

Reformatory School (1935-1948), an Institution for delinquent Africans, between about twelve and twenty-one years of age. We got on well and he agreed to let me come back another time and tape the interviews.

I understand that I was lucky to get this opportunity—indeed, I think I may have passed some private kind of test of his! I had been searching out the work of Can Themba, a Black writer who went into voluntary exile in Swaziland because of harassment by the South African Security Police. At the time, my friend Professor Donald Stuart and I had just made the first collection of Can's work to be published later (1972) in book form, under the title of *The Will To Die* in the Heinemann African Writers Series. I think *that* project may have had something to do with Paton's easy acceptance of me just then.

I saw Paton for the second time in June 1973, when I stayed in his house for about five days. The taped interviews were made on June 19 and June 20 of that year. The rest of the visit consisted mostly of conversations with the writer. The first visit consisted wholly of conversations—no taping was done then. The topics, on both occasions, were many and varied: about his political activities as well as his professional and personal life, but mainly about his work

On that second visit I was impressed by his concern to wake me gently by bringing tea each morning to my bedroom at about a quarter past seven. There are many other interesting recollections from both visits that I can recount.

For instance, one night at dinner, we were talking about his first wife, Dorrie's, illness. (Doris Olive Francis, whom he married at St. John's Anglican Church, Ixopo, on 2 July 1928. She died in 1967. He was still visibly affected when he told me of her death.) He said that smoking—a life long habit—had caused her emphysema. He pointed out that Cedric Hardwicke, the famous actor, had died of the same disease and it wasn't all that uncommon: the cells of the lungs begin to die off, he said, and it gradually encroaches on the whole lung. Once begun, it is irreversible, and his wife was breathing with less and less of her lung as time went on. In the last twelve months of her life, she lived entirely on oxygen. "It was a very distressing thing to watch," he said. (He added that his son, Jonathan, may have inherited some tendency, as he is rather "short of breath".)

Introduction

He mentioned that he had been deeply moved by reading C.S. Lewis's *A Grief Observed* and intended to write something of his own when he was better able to cope with his memories. (This intention saw the light of day, of course, as *Kontakion For One Departed.* published in 1969—titled *For You Departed* in the U.S.A.)

An anecdote, prompted by my telling him about some Achilles tendon trouble I had had after taking part in a hundred yards 'dash' for fathers on some celebratory day in Lesotho, goes as follows: He was thinking of marrying Anne (his second wife), so he thought he had better get fit. He was aged about 69 at this time. He went for a walk in some nearby woods and started jogging. He hadn't gone more than a few paces when his Achilles tendon went. "That was the end of my jogging," he said. He was obviously amused at himself while telling me this. It is an image that 'opens the door', a 'key' (his own word) to his personality. [See his comments on Jan Hofmeyr in *The Lintrose Conversations* below. Hofmeyr was one time Vice-Chancellor of the University of the Witwatersrand, Deputy Prime Minister under general Smuts, eminent administrator and liberal politician in South Africa. Paton's biography of him was published in 1964. Hofmeyr was appearing on a platform with General Smuts, at some public event. "Hoffie said to Paton, 'You know, he is not very much taller than I am, is he?'" Paton's comment was that Smuts was inches taller.]

Anne was probably his secretary in the last year of Dorrie's life, who was, according to Paton, bedridden and quite unable to do things. Anne said that when she came into the job, things were in a devil of a mess. I can only guess what she meant by this; but the probability is that, in the last year of Dorrie's life, Paton had little, if any, secretarial help, and Anne came on the scene after Dorrie had died (in1967), although Paton himself recollected some kind of an overlap.

He recounted an incident when Anne, and a male friend of hers, and he himself had arranged a night out together. They were to meet at Anne's house or flat. But "this chap didn't turn up!" Anne said they had better call it off, but Alan Paton said, "No, why should we? Let's go and eat." So he took her out to dinner. They had a nice meal: plenty of talk and so on.

I think it was on this occasion that the topic somehow arose of the possibility of his marrying again. He said that so far he had had no such thoughts, but—"well, if I did, it would be somebody like her."

3

Because of the way he had phrased it Anne interpreted this as a kind of proposal.

At the time, she was married. She also had children. However, her marriage was on the rocks—"about to break up"—Paton said. So a divorce came about. Whether it was pressed by Anne or Paton or Anne's husband, I do not know. Her husband was a Flying Officer in the RAF, who had been posted to South Africa. They came over in the sixties. Anne had been in the country about ten years.

Anyway, the next thing was that reporters came to see Paton. Gossip had somehow got around. They came to interview him, ostensibly, about his thoughts on his work. At the end of the interview someone asked, "Well, what about your future plans, Mr Paton?" He began to tell them about his writing plans. They said, "No, we don't mean *that*. We mean your personal plans." He replied, "How do you mean—'my personal plans'?" "Well," said one of them, "We've heard that you're going to get married again." So, resignedly, he said, "Oh well, if you have heard that much, I suppose so."

He seemed to imply that this was one of the reasons he made a statement to them. If things had got so far public, he felt he couldn't retract. Thus, he gave out the news that he was about to be married. Soon after, Anne and he *were* married.

I may have picked up the wrong impression from him then, but it sounded that, on his part, it was more a marriage of respect than of love. Clearly, this later changed. But, at this time, a lot of the moving force seems to have come from Anne. My impressions could be quite wrong. Because, he said very sincerely, it was one of the best things he had ever done in his life, and he was very glad that he was married to Anne. "She is a very fine woman," he said.

He spoke Zulu to Theresa and his other servants. Theresa is the one who brought his tea and laid the table. Mrs Paton told me that Theresa was 'getting on' and was becoming very forgetful. At dinner one night, she forgot the serving spoons, the serving knives and forks, and some other item. Very gently, I heard him tell her that she was now "pensionable" and she had better "watch out!" It was all in good fun.

Anne had two Dalmatians, which absolutely adored her. They spent their time outside, unless she was in the house, and then they came in. She gave the younger animal some kind of a sweetmeat every night. She told it to lie down and when it was flat, (they said "Flat!"), then they gave it the sweetmeat. They had a very corpulent cat also; a large thing called Tosca. It was as big as a Scotch terrier, I suppose, extremely spoilt: it mewed to come in at night, and once it was in, it mewed to go out! But it was a friendly and appealing animal.

The only time Paton could recall that he had been bothered by the Special Branch was at the time of the Defence and Aid scheme. [The South African Defence and Aid Fund was established by liberals in 1960. It gave succour to those charged with political offences. It was banned under the Suppression of Communism Act in 1966.] This was when he lived at Kloof, I think; or maybe at Anerley—one of the two. His house was searched. But he said that it was a very perfunctory affair, really. The whole thing took about two hours. They came into the room and looked at his books. And one of the men said, "I have got the book, the book!"—"*Ek het die boek, die boek!*" He didn't know whether the policeman meant that Paton had so many books; or whether he was simply astounded; or that they *had* to search the books *individually*.

Anyway he told them where to look and where to find the papers they wanted. He didn't obstruct them in any way, but he commented on their progress: "I don't mind if you waste your time or not, but you won't find anything in that drawer." Or that drawer! Or that drawer! And so on. Then he took them to his study and he said, "There is nothing here. This is where I do my writing." They took his word for it.

He said the sitting room in that house was a very peculiar shape, and two people could sit in one corner and not be seen by anybody in the rest of the room. There seemed to be three of four corners like this. When it came time for Paton and his wife to take tea, they sat in a place which was hidden from view. But the two Special Branch men came and sat with them. This annoyed the Patons.

Someone else being searched by the Security Police, at the same time—I think he may have said it was Peter Brown [Liberal Party formed in 1953; Brown opened the first party office in Pietermaritzburg, became National Chairman in 1958, imprisoned in 1960, banned for five years in 1964]—underwent quite a different procedure. The Special Branch spent two or three days turning his whole place upside down.

I asked Paton if he thought his telephone was tapped. He replied, "Oh yes, I have almost no doubt about it." And his mail? He thought this was also watched, because he had replied to letters which nobody ever received. But, on the whole, he was left alone.

His book sales were quite staggering. In the USA in 1972, he still sold 70 000 copies a year of *Cry, the Beloved Country* [first published in 1948], and the sales of that novel, he said, "made everything else possible." He estimated that he may have sold between 5 and 6 million copies of that work in all!

He mentioned that there had been a symposium on South African literature in 1968 or 1969, in Durban, where a Professor Grobbelar was present, who claimed that *Cry, The Beloved Country* had got no merit at all! The Professor claimed that it could have been written by a matriculation level student [College entrant]! Paton's reply, according to him, ran along the lines of: "If it could have been done by a student, it is a pity that 'our Professor Grobbelar' had not written it himself at the time! He may have been in quite a different position now!" A rather petty squabble, I thought!

In almost the same breath he mentioned a South African writer called G H Kalpin who, he said, wasn't financially very successful. Apparently, when asked about the Professor's remark, he gave a reply to the effect that "Mr Paton knew how to make money."

I think it was in relation to this particular symposium that an inhabitant of Durban, an Indian woman who appears to have been a life-long friend (whom he didn't mention by name), attacked him in a letter, calling him, he implied, 'a traitor to the cause,' or something of the kind. She had persuaded her brother to take this letter (to which he had managed to append about twenty-five other signatures) to the editor of a Durban paper, the *Sunday Tribune* in Natal. This editor informed Paton of the letter and asked him what he would do about it. The whole episode had hurt Paton deeply. His usual practice was not to answer criticisms in the press. He departed from his routine this time by writing this lady a personal letter. Neither her letter or his has been published; he wouldn't mention any names. He said it was another example of the attacks on liberals and liberalism that occur all the time.

Another comment on a writer which he did not want noted at the time: he could "see nothing" in the stories of Joy Packer (a popular

South African novelist of his era). But I believe he had first made the comment in 1968 or 9.

I asked him why his books had so many publishers. The first book, *Cry, the Beloved Country*, was taken by Cape: then, when he wanted them to take *Hofmeyr*, Ron Howard, who had died, was replaced by someone else, and it was turned down. Afterwards, Cape wanted to know why he hadn't offered it to them. Paton said, "Well, I did offer it to you." Cape said, "We know nothing about that." He had already offered *Hofmeyr* [1964] to OUP, who took it. [In the U.S. the book was titled *South African Tragedy: The Life and Times of Jan Hofmeyr*, Scribners, 1965.]

Scribners, his American publishers, "took everything." They also wanted his biography of Clayton. This book, which he was working on when I interviewed him in June of 1973, *Apartheid and the Archbishop*, a biography of Geoffrey Clayton, Archbishop of Cape Town, he had decided to give to a new South African publisher, David Phillip of Cape Town, and it was to be published in September of 1973. Then, too (in 1973), he understood that Jonathan Cape wanted the projected biography of Roy Campbell; so, apparently, did OUP.

The book of meditations he produced, *Instrument of Thy Peace* [1968], was a commission for Seaberry. *Kontakion For You Departed* published by Jonathan Cape in 1969, was brought out by Scribners under its American title of *For One Departed. The Land and People of South Africa* (aimed at high school students in the UK and USA.1955) was done by Lippincote, an American publisher now defunct. (He suggested that somebody brought the latter book up to date.) He had no binding contract with any of the publishers for all his books.

In our discussions on the topic of writing biography, it was his opinion that people should not write the biographies of those still living. In his opinion, it is impossible to tell the whole truth about a living person. He mentioned his experience with the writing of *Hofmeyr*. Then, the "Old Lady" (as he called her) was still alive. He put it aside for six months or a year, because she didn't like the way it was going. [He took it up again in1959, when the "Old Lady" died.]

He had the same feelings about the projected biography of Roy Campbell. Mary, Campbell's wife, was still alive in 1973. This was one reason he put the Campbell biography away in 1970. He wrote the biography of Geoffrey Clayton instead. (When I asked him, at some point, if I could do *his* biography, he mentioned his own "putting off" of the Campbell project, and seemed to suggest that I wouldn't be able to tell the whole truth about *him*.)

For one of the tapes, I asked him about The Rev Charles Hooper as a possible subject for a biography. At that point, he asked me to switch off the tape recorder. He didn't want to go on record with the following remarks. (But after such a long time, I don't think there can be anything against reporting his comments.) He thought that Charles Hooper "was certainly not a Great Man." He thought that Hooper was, in fact, "driven by something other than Goodness." But he "didn't want to imply that Hooper was driven by Evil." He suggested that the kind of impulse and motive he found in people like Trevor Huddleston [priest of the Anglican Community of the Resurrection who worked for Africans at the Rosettenville Mission House, Johannesburg, and was the model for Father Vincent in *Cry, the Beloved Country,* who wrote *Naught For Your Comfort,* and later became Bishop of Masasi, Tanzania] and the Reverend Michael Scott [who appeared repeatedly before the U.N. Fourth Trusteeship Committee on behalf of the Hereros of former South West Africa, and joined the Passive Resistance Movement against the Asiatic Land tenure Act of South Africa, and who went to prison in 1946, barred from South Africa as a 'prohibited immigrant' in 1952, and who wrote *A Time to Speak* in 1958] and Archbishop Clayton certainly wasn't present in Hooper.. He said, quite categorically, The Reverend Hooper was slightly unhinged!

We also had a long discussion about Bishop Reeves (Ambrose Reeves, Anglican Bishop of Johannesburg, who was deported from South Africa in 1960). He thought that Reeves was quite decidedly not a Great Man. Reeves left South Africa for Swaziland to escape the Special Branch.[1]

---

[1] At a time when the Apartheid South African Government was rounding up thousands of all races, had declared a State of Emergency and was about to outlaw the ANC, the Bishop left for Swaziland – immediately to escape being silenced by the police and then, when he went on to England, where he had been due to spend long leave, to speak out. His departure caused much controversy. It is significant that those most bitterly critical were white members of his diocese and of the clergy who had most disapproved of him, or resented autocratic treatment, while African and left-wing comment was sympathetic. He

Introduction

First, he told me of events behind that occurrence.

One night he got a phone call; from his daughter-in-law (or one of his daughters). The phone call said that the Special Branch was going to arrest both Paton and Reeves. He was advised to get out of the country. He talked this over with his wife, Dorrie. They sat up most of the night discussing it. In the end, they decided that he wouldn't leave, but just sit it out and see what would happen. It was Paton's belief that Special Branch was simply trying to scare them and so wouldn't really do anything. Also, he believed that it was his duty to stay in South Africa.

Reeves, he claimed, abandoned his duty as a Priest. He maintained that Bishops and Archbishops take a vow that they will never desert their flocks. (He tried to find this in a book of prayer, but could not put his finger on it.) He maintained, however, that there *was* such a vow.

Anyway, Reeves deserted to Swaziland and Alan Paton went there to look for him. When he arrived, he phoned Reeves and said, "This is Alan Paton speaking." Archbishop Reeves wouldn't believe him. He thought it was a hoax of the Special Branch. It took Paton two hours, by phoning and phoning, to convince Reeves that it *was* Paton. He went there to try to persuade Reeves to come back. I asked Paton why he thought Reeves had gone to Swaziland, in the first place. He replied that it was "perfectly simple"—"Reeve's wife had threatened him that if he didn't go to Swaziland, she would divorce him! And, of course, it was unthinkable that a man in his position in the Church could be divorced!"

Paton flew back from Swaziland in a private plane, which lost its bearings in mist. It came down some thirty miles from Pietermaritzburg, in a field. The passengers were given food and shelter in a nearby house, then finally made their way back to Pietermaritzburg.

The Special Branch never appeared, which confirmed Alan Paton's view that it had all been a kind of psychological tactic on the part of the Special Branch and that there had been no intention to arrest either Reeves or himself.

---

returned to South Africa in September 1960, and two days later the Security Police, without charge or trial, deported him.

He thought this incident altered Reeves very radically. Paton saw him again, in 1971, in Britain, and "He wasn't the same man. He was a very, very sad man indeed." Paton believed it was "this dereliction of duty" that caused it. And Paton surmised that it would have made Reeves' marriage worse—although he didn't suggest the marriage would break up. Reeves' wife was obviously not the kind of dedicated liberal that Dorrie, Paton's wife, was. Perhaps Reeves' wife gave preference to personal before other values. I put it to Paton that it was a very difficult decision that Reeves had had to make. That all organisation, faiths and ideologies were there to improve human life, in some way, was a truism. Nevertheless, what happened between individuals, between people—personal relationships—was what really mattered, wasn't it? If you had a situation which brought structures and personal values into conflict, one had to decide whether to destroy one's own personal love, or that of a bigger group: *that* was a real conflict. I didn't know what I would do. Alan Paton said that he was quite clear what he would do.

This discussion brought to my mind a story by Nadine Gordimer, which is about a man who is Head of a Reformatory. He is so taken up by his job and what he has to do that he completely neglects his wife. It occurred to me that it is probably based on Alan Paton, not that there was any question at all of Alan Paton neglecting his own wife. The neglect of the wife of the story was an imaginative invention, and has no basis in fact. (It would be interesting, sometime, to confirm my guess with Nadine Gordimer!)

From there he went on to talk about books which had impressed him. A book that he said is rarely heard of "now" (1973), called *They Sat Down and Wept by Grand Central Station* by the Canadian author Elizabeth Smart (published in 1945) is the only novel he has ever read twice. He had got a great respect and admiration for it. When he was about thirty-one, he read a novel called *Death Comes to the Archbishop* (published in 1927) by Willa Cather, about the attempts of a Catholic bishop and a priest to establish a diocese in New Mexico Territory. The book impressed him very much at the time. He read it again about ten years later, when he was forty-one, but it didn't have anything like the same impact. Another book he mentioned as being one "he liked" was: *The Bridge of San Louis Rey* by Thornton Wilder. He had tried to read *USA* by John Dos Passos, but couldn't. He mentioned that Jean Paul Sartre thought that this was "a very great

Introduction

book." When I mentioned that F R Leavis also thought highly of it, he said that he would "have another go at it." In talking about *Lord Jim* by Joseph Conrad, he only got part of the way when he first tried to read it, and stopped. The second time, he got half way through when suddenly the thing "clicked." He had found an essay by Langston Hughes very interesting; it examined how the words 'black' and 'white' were used in the language. "Black, the Ace of Spades, was associated with evil, and white with some kind of purity," had stuck firmly in his mind. (See Hughes' essay 'The Negro Artist and the Racial Mountain,' published in *The Nation* in 1926.)

He talked about the men who had had the greatest influences on the twentieth century: four names could not be left out of the list, he thought, *viz.* Darwin, Marx, Freud and Einstein. He had a great admiration for the film, *Oh What a Lovely War*—the only film he had seen twice. His bedtime reading would be somebody like Agatha Christie or Neville Shute. He read fairly widely and indiscriminately, and enjoyed light literature.

I made a note of some of the books in his study. He had the two-volume edition of Webster's *Third International Dictionary,* and the *Shorter Oxford* in one volume. He had a well-worn edition of the *Encyclopaedia Britannica*, which he said he would not be without. (His wife suggested that he got rid of this set and bought a new one.) On a bookshelf immediately behind his desk, he had all his own titles, in American, British and foreign language editions. He had quite a considerable number of novels around, and lots of history books and a good number of 'Afrikaner' books. On a bookshelf facing him, on the top and second shelf, he had placed the books he needed for the Campbell biography he had been working on

There were also photographs of people he liked to be reminded of: one or two of Hofmeyr; one of Jan Smuts among a group of people; a portrait of a black boy from Diepkloof (I think taken by Tom Sharp, the photographer). And immediately behind him, on the top shelf of the bookshelves containing his own works, there was a photograph of Albert Luthuli. [Chief Albert Luthuli was President of the Africa National Congress, and was awarded the Nobel Prize for Peace in 1961. He wrote *Let My People Go*, McGraw Hill, 1962. When a tombstone was unveiled for the great leader in July 1972, at Groutville, Paton was asked to give a memorial speech, which is published as 'Memorial to Luthuli.']

In his study, Paton had a kist that contained manuscripts, some of which he had even forgotten about. The MSS of the novel he once intended to write about a character called "Retief" (a symbolic representation of Christ) was "in there somewhere." He was going to show it to me but he couldn't put his hand on it. He had all the Hofmeyr MSS in there; and "God knows what else." His wife didn't know, and neither did he. His manuscripts of *Cry, the Beloved Country* and *Too Late the Phalarope*, he had lent to the University of the Witwatersrand; they had had them for some years. But he stressed that he had only *lent* them.

In 1973 he was awarded three honorary doctorates, one being from Yale, another from Edinburgh. Yale paid his first class airfare (by Concorde!), and his hotel was arranged and booked for him. Everything was done for him, in fact. There, he had a lucrative Chubb fellowship, at Timothy and Dwight College, and during his stay he needn't have given any lectures but "more or less made himself available." He gave an address at Yale. In Edinburgh he said there was no hotel put on, no arrangements made, and all his expenses he paid himself. (Casual treatment for a world figure, I thought!)

With regard to his address at the University of Yale in 1973, a girl in the audience stood up and asked him why he was so optimistic about South Africa. He said that he didn't think that he was being optimistic: he had simply tried to put the pros and cons as honestly as he could. But, he pointed out, he would obviously be worried if she thought that he hadn't answered the question properly. On reflection, he thought the "right" answer would have been the following. If anybody (he postulated) ten years ago, having read all about the history of Europe since the Middle Ages, with all its wars and bloodshed, and so on, had had the temerity to suggest that the Common Market was a possibility, he would have been laughed at. Could you predict, from the history of Europe, the Common Market? "Of course, you couldn't." This was, he thought, maybe the right kind of answer about South Africa, at the time.

He told me about a reading in Grahamstown, Eastern Cape, South Africa (he didn't specify dates), where both he and Nadine Gordimer had performed. He asked me to switch off the tape recorder at this point, as he had no wish to be reported. However, now it is a matter of literary history and no harm will result from reporting it. The matter has, in any case, already been mentioned by Stephen Gray [a South African scholar, writer and critic].

Nadine Gordimer read a story, and he read some extract from *Kontakian for One Departed.* She got hardly any applause at all; it simply didn't go across to the audience. Whereas the applause that he got was "overwhelming." He found this most uncomfortable. "Nobody wants to hog the stage. I would be very careful who I performed with next time." Those were his exact words. He made the point about her writing being "clinical." He said that "she was like a spectator looking down on the arena all the time, and seeing everything. But she wasn't involved." He was actively *there*, in the centre, doing things.

At just about the time of my second visit to him, Nadine Gordimer had recently published *The Conservationist.* I told him I thought it was her best novel so far; at least, it was the one I liked best. He had also read it and liked it. He told me he had telephoned to congratulate her on the novel. He said, among other things, that he thought it had "more heart" than her earlier work. She said, "Alan, that is not what I'm about." He replied, "Nadine, there is nothing else! There is nothing else, Nadine!"

At the time he also mentioned an article by Christina van Heyningen, which appeared in *Theoria.*[2]

I think it was on my first visit that I asked him, from sheer curiosity, how he had lost the second finger of his left hand. This was at Diepkloof Reformatory, when some big African came at him, and he hit this chap in the mouth. [The inmates ranged from about thirteen to twenty-one years old.] He said he must have had bad teeth because, afterwards, his finger began to swell: it was painful and took a long time healing. When it eventually healed, it was completely rigid. He couldn't bend it at all. "It got in the way;" so he decided to have it off. I asked him if this had been any inconvenience to him and he said, no, not at all—except he couldn't play cricket properly! "I couldn't hold a bat."

He was a small man, I should think about 5 ft 4 or 5, possibly 5ft 6. At the time of the interview (June 19-20 1973), he looked very much older than when I saw him three years before—and fuller. He had even

---

[2] I can't remember if this was an article about him; or one about a talk on Roy Campbell he had given somewhere – Roy Holland.

acquired a 'tub.' He was an endearing man. He was telling me that Anne had rationed him to six cigarettes a night. It used to be nine: he had managed to cut it down by three. When he finished work for the day he usually had a whisky, which he drank rather quickly. He said this did something to his "taste buds" so that he could appreciate a cigarette. Before that, it was repellent to him. He didn't smoke at all in the daytime. Then, at night, he had the six cigarettes—no more, no less. He took two or three whiskies before he ate; and he liked to have wine with his evening meal as well.

When he was amused—which was not rare—he had a smile which lit up his whole being. He looked thirty years younger: all the wrinkles of age went away, the shape of his face seemed to return to when he was about forty. He just completely lit up! It was such a contrast to the grim expressions he habitually wore… Were they some kind of camouflage?

Another thing I want to record (trivial but interesting) are details about his straw hats. He wore a very wide-brimmed rather flat variety—like those a French priest wears—only in straw. He always wore one when he was out in the sun and he had several of them (three perhaps) lying around the house. But he seemed to utilize only one of them: the other two or three, in various stages of antiquity—holes in them and fraying—he nevertheless kept.

In about a month's time he was going to Portugal to see Mary Campbell to ask her more questions for the biography of Roy Campbell he was collecting material on. Then he was going on to the U.K to meet his wife, who was travelling on ahead of him.

This is the point from which the interview follows.

Roy Holland
Ledbury, Herefordshire
June 2008

THE LINTROSE CONVERSATIONS
Interview with Alan Paton
19th and 20th June 1973

The actual discussions. These interviews were recorded on 19 and 20 June 1973 in Alan Paton's house, Botha's Hill, Kloof, Natal. The name of his house was Lintrose. Therefore, these interviews are called *The Lintrose Conversations*. The questions were spontaneous, and followed, as far as possible, the directions he wished to take. I merely wished to record as much information as I could on the topics discussed.

RH: "Could you tell me where you learnt Afrikaans?"

AP: "Oh yes."

RH: "At home, or in school?"

AP: "When I was young—in school—I was in [Zululand]. It wasn't until I started teaching that I decided to become bilingual. I was teaching in the [Ixopo High School] at that time. I went off with the Afrikaans master. Went to a remote place in the Boland,

and I stayed there with his family. I wasn't able [allowed] to speak a word of English, and in a matter of a month or so, I had to speak Afrikaans the whole time. I had a sort of a headache for about a week and suddenly—KATTOU! Well then, when I came back, I was officially bilingual; but really, I became bilingual when I went to Diepkloof Reformatory [1935] when I was thirty-two. Because there my white staff was almost entirely Afrikaans speaking."

RH: "And that was about 1935, wasn't it?"

AP: "1935, yes. And the boys, delinquent boys, their language was Afrikaans—delinquent black boys in South Africa. Those who came from Natal—their delinquent language wasn't English, it was Zulu; but in Johannesburg, Pretoria, Bloemfontein, every other town, it was Afrikaans."

RH: "And you are quite fluent in Zulu as well, aren't you?"

AP: "Not as fluent as I am in Afrikaans. I talked more Afrikaans for thirteen years [at Diepkloof] than I talked English."

RH: "Extraordinary, and now you are at home in both languages?"

AP: "Yes, except that, living as I do now in Natal, in this particular part of Natal [Botha's Hill], one very seldom gets the opportunity to speak Afrikaans."

RH: "And could you tell me the schools you attended, with the year?"

AP: "Yes. I went to Berg Street Girls School when I was six. That was 1909. And then in 1910 I went to [Ablock Road], which was a new school which opened in 1910. In 1914 I went to 'Maritzburg

College till 1918. In 1919 I went to the Natal University College and left that in the middle of 1924."

RH: "And at Natal you did Maths and Physics, didn't you?"

AP: "I did Maths and Physics, yes."

RH: "And what was your first job, after that?"

AP: "My first job was to teach for two months at Newcastle High School. I taught Standard Four. Only as a sort of a fill-up job, and I started the new year at Ixopo."

RH: "And were you there for four years?"

AP: "Three and a half."

RH: "For three and a half, and there seems to be some conflict in the sources I consulted, about what kind of a school it was then. According to Current Biography it says that it was a Zulu school."

AP: "Oh no! No, that's quite wrong! It was a *white* school, and it was just in the process of becoming a High School. I really went there to teach the first Standard Nine. And the next year came the first Standard Ten, and after that it was a fully-fledged High School. And it grew so big that today the High School is totally separated from the Primary School."

RH: "And your second job—was that at Pietermaritzburg College?"

AP: "Yes."

RH: "For seven years?"

AP: "From the middle of 1928 to the middle of 1935—seven years."

RH: "Now, just to move away from that, in 'A School in Danger,' you showed there, your interest in Adams College. I wondered how you first became interested in it and how you first struck up your friendship with Father Huddleston?"

AP "Oh well, those are two separate questions."

RH: "Yes, they are."

AP: "When I was a schoolmaster at 'Marizburg College, we took a cricket team, not an official cricket team, down to Adams College to play against them. I suppose that was one of my first ventures into that sort of field. They put books first. Then, the Principal—I cannot remember whether he made the suggestion to me, or if I made it to him—I cannot remember—but we went down there and we slept there the night. It was the first experience that these White boys had had of that. And it really was also the first experience that these Black boys had had of it, too.

Now your second question, about Father Huddleston. When I was at Diepkloof Reformatory we also had a cricket team. We used to play against St. Peter's School, which was run by the Community of the Resurrection, and we had been playing them for some years, six or seven years; and then Father Huddleston arrived and then went on to become the Prior. And that is how I came to strike up a friendship with Father Huddleston."

RH: "Through cricket?"

AP: "Well through—By going to the school, to the Community of the Resurrection."

RH: "I see, yes. Now, I think it was in 1935, you went to Diepkloof. How did it come about that you left the teaching profession to go to the Reformatory School?"

AP: "In 1934 the South African Parliament transferred all Reformatories from the Department of Prisons to the Department of Education, and I thought that I would like to try a job like this. So I wrote to Mr Hofmeyr, who was the Minister of Education, and told him I would like to try a Reformatory job. I had no intention of going to Diepkloof. Well, he said, "Apply for the whole lot"—which I did, and then to my astonishment, I got Diepkloof."

RH: "Yes, I think that you mentioned it in *Hofmeyr,* didn't you, in the biography?"

AP: "I don't think in *Hofmeyr.*"

RH: "I recall some mention of it somewhere."

AP: "Maybe, I mentioned it in *Kontakion For One Departed?*"

RH: "Ah, was that it?"

AP: "I take myself out of *Hofmeyr,* as far as possible. I don't think that it would be in there, somehow."

RH: "No, maybe it would have been documented as a letter or something of that kind?"

AP: "I didn't get Diepkloof Reformatory letters."

RH: "Now I think it would be interesting to—"

AP: "You'll be interested enough that in *Hofmeyr*, I kept myself out of it altogether and never used 'I' or 'myself.' I always used 'the biographer,' 'the writer.' 'Alan Paton' I used for the rest of it.

RH: "I see. Why was that?"

AP: "I decided—discussed it with my son, Jonathan, and discussed it with Tony Norfolk in Durban. I discussed it with several of my friends who said that—I have a feeling that it belongs to a past era—to keep on saying 'the writer,' 'the biographer' when you really mean yourself. And especially when you have been involved in the man's life."

RH: "Yes."

AP: "I just gave it up in time."

RH: "Yes, a slightly more personal narrative."

AP: "One gets used to it in the end."

RH: "Is it correct that when the Second World War broke out you wished to do military service, backed by the Government?"

AP: "Yes, that's correct."

RH: "How did you feel at that time?"

AP: "I felt very strongly about Hitler, if that's what you mean, until they said 'You stay where you are,' and I did."

RH: "Now, when you were at Diepkloof – you have already answered my next question about the Afrikaners you met there – but I think that it is being claimed that your experience there enabled you to portray at least two characters in *Cry, the Beloved Country*. Is that correct?"

AP: "Which two?"

RH: "Now, that I don't know. I can't find out. It was only a mention in an essay I read by Richard Dale."

AP: "Yes, well, it is true. One was the young man who worked at the Reformatory, who was modelled, not on myself, as some people think, but on a young man who did work there. The old man, the old Kumalo, wasn't really modelled on anybody I knew; but the fact that the hero of the book was a priest, was very largely due to the fact that a very humble old priest used to come and see his son at Diepkloof. Naturally, one is moved to reflect upon the fact that here is this old man who is a priest in the Church, and his boy is an inmate in a Reformatory. And I presume, too, that it showed some—well, he was a very humble man—but it showed an even greater humility that he would humble himself to the extent that he would come out there in his priest clothes to see his boy."

RH: "So you wouldn't agree with the critics who say that Arthur Jarvis reflects your own personality pretty closely?"

AP: "Oh well, you can't argue about that, it did. But you are talking about another character, aren't you?"

RH: "Yes."

AP "Well, I mean, I used him as a mouthpiece, if that's what you mean. I think that I probably thought more highly of him than I thought of myself, if you understand."

RH: "Now, I think this is off on another tack. I am afraid I haven't followed any particular line in these questions, but it is clear to me that you grew up in a devoutly Christian home. Now I wonder if you could say a little bit about the kind of Christian observances."

AP: "I'll tell you what I am going to do. I had better give you a copy of this pamphlet. [I think this was 'Case History of a Pinky' published by the South African Institute of Race Relations in 1971 as 'Topical Talks' 28.] I'll give you a copy of it. It will answer your questions."

RH: "Ah, thank you. Oh, yes."

AP: "Have you got it?"

RH: "No, I had noted it, but I haven't got it. That's fine. Thank you. And does this say how you became interested in Toc-H?"[Talbot House War Services, a voluntary organization that helped members of the armed forces, like the help given by the Red Cross all over the world.]

AP: "No, I don't think so. I tell you, there was a reason for that."

RH: "Yes."

AP: "I was an Honorary Commissioner at Toc-H."

RH: "How did that come about?"

AP: "Well, Hofmeyr died and I was then sort of in the news, so they made me an Honorary Commissioner in, I think about 1949, probably. And then, in 1954[3] the Liberal Party started, and my

---

[3] Actually in 1953. See later referece.

fellow members of Toc-H were not excited about their Honorary Commissioner being a member of the Liberal Party [The LP was totally multiracial]; but if I had been a member of the United Party they wouldn't have worried at all; in fact, Hofmeyr was a member. There was even a Cabinet Minister in the U.P (United Party), but no, the Liberal Party, no! So I offered my resignation to them and they accepted it. So that is why you won't find any great enthusiasm for Toc-H."

RH: "Do you still have any connections with Toc-H?"

AP: "I'm what they call a general member, but they are still wrestling with the 'race business' in Toc H. There still are White members of Toc-H who don't want any non-racialism in Toc-H. We started fighting for this as far back as 1930-something, I would think. And now, forty years later, we have made some small steps forward.

RH: "But you really receive their literature, I suppose, and that's about all."

AP: "Yes, I do. Well, I was asked the other day to go and speak, and it is very rarely that I would be asked to speak in the first place; but I can assure you, I will take a long time in doing so, unless I was going there to tell them what I think. I don't believe in being diplomatic about a thing like that in an organisation which professes to be a Christian organisation."

RH: "Now you mentioned this, this morning, and I wondered if you could give me a little more on it—the novel that you were once working on, which was about the Second Coming of Christ, is that correct?"

AP: "That is putting it rather strongly. It was really the story of a young Afrikaner who comes to Johannesburg. He certainly has the gift of healing, and he also begins to transgress against the laws of the country—doesn't take any regard of the colour bar—goes to places he shouldn't go to without a Permit." [Because of the Group Areas Act 1950-1957, which governed where you could live. A White needed a Permit to go into a Black area, and a Black needed a Permit to go into a White residential area.]

RH: "Was there any direct parallel in your mind at the time between character…?"

AP: "And?"

RH: "And the Christ?"

AP: "Oh yes. I cannot remember, now, why I gave it up—whether I gave it up because I thought, well, it was a bit too complex."

RH: "You say that you couldn't remember now why you gave it up. Do you remember what happened to the manuscript?"

AP: "I suspect it's in that tin. [He points to the kist. We are in his study]. I'll get my wife to have a look."

RH: "And was there another novel that you had begun before Diepkloof, that you didn't complete? I've seen it said that there were two that you started before."

AP: "Ah, yes, but I told you about that this morning. Well, that was when I was a schoolmaster in my early twenties, I should think."

RH: "What was that about?"

AP: "It was about Ixopo life, and they were influenced, I think, by [Hugh] Walpole, [who wrote] the *Rogue Herries* series of novels, things like that. You see, in the old days, in Ixopo, they had some wild customers about. Some of those early settlers were very wild men; they reminded me very much of the characters in *Rogue Herries*. But, you see, I'm already beginning to concern myself about the problems of Order and Justice, and *Rogue Herries* was fine, but it didn't really belong; and I think that's why I finally decided to throw it away."

RH: "It didn't in fact carry what you wanted?"

AP: "I think that I would find it very difficult to write a story that didn't have some kind of a social meaning. Not because I believe that a story should have a social meaning at all, but it is just what one's nature is, one's character is."

RH: "It doesn't engage you properly unless it has?"

AP: "That's true. I will always say and you will see when you read this review [I think this was a review of the Afrikaans novel *Na die Geliefde Land* by Karel Schoeman, that Paton had just written, 1973], a writer may have two purposes. His one purpose is to tell a story, but he may also have a second purpose; he may want to teach a lesson. But the second purpose—he may want to teach a lesson—must never overwhelm the first purpose. What is more, the second purpose must never become visible. The reader must never think, 'Ah, this book is trying to teach me a lesson.' But nevertheless, I have no doubt that a good story can teach you lessons."[His ideas can be read formulated in his 'Some Thoughts on the Contemporary Novel in Afrikaans,' 1959, and in 'The South African Novel in English,' 1956.]

RH: "Would it be true to say, then, Mr Paton, when you began in your twenties, you thought of yourself more as a novelist than as a general writer?"

AP: "Yes, I think that would be true."

RH: "What happened?"

AP: "Well, I suppose Diepkloof would be the big thing. Joining the Institute of Race Relations—all in that book. Joining the Institute of Race Relations, being on Bishop Clayton's Commission during the war. Helping him to found, and joining the Liberal Party, and through those things."

RH: "Do you regret that you haven't written more novels, or do you think that you have said your say?"

AP: "I would still like to write a novel."

RH: "Do you have one planned?"

AP: "You see, when Professor W. H. Gardner died, I said to his son, Professor Colin Gardner, 'Now who is going to write [the biography of] Roy Campbell?' and he said he didn't know, 'there's all the material there.' His father had done a lot of work, and I said, 'Well, if I had the time I wouldn't mind having a go at it myself; but I was already started on [the life of Bishop] Clayton, at that time.'

Well, I think biography is very satisfying, but it's a different type of creation. I wouldn't like to suggest that one writes biography because it is easier to write than fiction. Because, as I was telling you this morning, there is one way in which it is easier, and there is one way in which it is much more difficult. The one way in which it is easier is that you already have a theme, so you can't go wrong. You've got the life of a man in front of you. The way in which it is more difficult is that you are bound by facts; you can't use your imaginative faculties to the same extent as you do when writing a novel, and part of the great enjoyment of writing a story is using your imaginative faculty. That doesn't mean to say that your imaginative faculty doesn't get used. Because, in trying to recreate a man's life, you have to put yourself into it."

RH: "Do you have another novel in mind?"

AP: "I would like to write another novel about South Africa. I can't say that I've got a specific thing in mind."

RH: "This is about *Too Late the Phalarope*. Your portrayal in there of Mathew Kaplan, a Jewish shopkeeper, showed a good deal of understanding and compassion and respect for the Jewish community of South Africa. I wondered what connections, personal or social, you've had with the Jewish community of South Africa?"

AP: "Well, in the first place, we were not brought up to be anti-Semitic, in the fact that Jesus was a Jew—a very important fact. I think that would be one reason. I think the other reason is that when you are beginning to break down barriers between yourself and the Afrikaner, or yourself and the African, and in the end everything breaks—all barriers break down. Any racial generalisation, you just throw it all together. In the first place, because it is likely to be wrong, and in the second place because it portrays, as Campbell does, in the autobiographies of his. It portrays that, when a fellow is a Jew, it is the first thing that Campbell thinks about. He always will tell you that he was a Jew. He never tells you that this chap was a—"

RH: "—person or a man."

AP: "And then, in the Johannesburg—. There was the Institute of Race Relations; and also, I joined the Society of Christians and Jews, in which Hoernlé [Alfred Hoernlé, Professor of Philosophy at the University of the Witwatersrand from 1923 to 1943, who, together with his wife, founded the Institute of Race Relations] and

Clayton were prominent figures; and then, finally, the Liberal Party. There was also a large strong Jewish element—and, of course, Hitler also confirmed me."

RH: "You have already mentioned, in passing, the number of social organisations of one kind or another that you have been concerned with, the organisation of social services, and so on. Are there any others that you haven't mentioned which played an important part in your life?"

AP: "There are some others that I played an important part in, such as, for example, what was called the Non-European Association of Boys Clubs—which I did a great deal of work for, about, I would think, eleven or more years. I have already told you about Toc-H. I've been a member of the Institute [of Race Relations] since about 1935, I think. I was a member of the Liberal Party."

RH: "Botha's Hill?"[Most car drivers in South Africa would know Botha's Hill, Natal, a long dangerous incline on the main road to Durban, as an accident blackspot. The name also refers to a residential village where Paton lived, and its accompanying postal area. When I stayed with him in his residence, *Lintrose,* I was conscious of the dull roar of the traffic noise from this route all the time. A large volume of cars and heavy vehicles use it constantly. Twenty years earlier, in 1953, when the Patons were presumably living at Kloof, a few miles away from Botha's Hill, just after *Too Late the Phalarope* was published, AP worked with his wife for a year at the Toc-H TB settlement in Botha's Hill, helping cured African patients to return to normal life.]

AP: "*Ja,* well, that is not an organisation. I went there because I was a member of Toc-H. You see, because the chap in charge of it was Don Mackenzie, who was a friend of mine in Toc-H. And that was before I offered my resignation; because then that [problem] really came up over the Liberal Party."

RH: "Now you also mentioned the South African Institute of Race Relations, (SAIRR), and you are a member of that. Do you have any other connections with them and so forth? I know you have written pamphlets for them."

AP: "Do you mean any Office?"

RH: "Yes."

AP: "No. I think that there were people in the Institute of Race Relations who also looked askance [at the Liberal Party]. See, that is the whole conflict between the Pietist and the Activist, and I am very much an Activist—I have got no use for Pietism when it is divorced from Activity—and you get this in any organisation."

RH: "So you gave your support in theory, as it were, without being wholehearted?"

AP: "In the Institute?"

RH: "Yes."

AP: "Oh no, I was very active in the Institute in my Johannesburg days. I never sought office in the Institute, and somewhere, about twenty-three years ago, Mrs Hoernlé [Winifred] asked me to give the Hoernlé lecture, and I couldn't do it at that time. The invitation was never renewed. For twenty-three years they had all sorts of speakers giving the Hoernlé lecture. If they were to ask me to do it today, I would be very reluctant."

RH: "Why is that?"

AP: "Well, I don't look kindly on people who throw their skirts aside when we at the Liberal Party were trying to do what we thought was the right thing. We were trying to get political expression.

Quite frankly my opinion of those who drew aside, didn't rise. I must also admit that very often when people try to make a reparation, it is not always the same people who drew aside."

RH: "Yes, I can see that. Now I would like to ask you something about your writing of the novel *Cry, the Beloved Country*. I believe you told me last time that you wrote part of it in Scandinavia."

AP: "Yes, that's true."

RH: "I think that you wrote part of it in Father Huddleston's house, is that correct? It has been quoted as being so."

AP: "*He* wrote part of *his* book in *my* house."

RH: "Is that the way around, is it?"

AP "Yes, he wrote part of *Naught For Your Comfort*—in my house."

RH: "I see, that must have been a mistake."

AP: "Very much a mistake."

RH: "In what other places did you write *Cry, the Beloved Country*?"

AP: "I started it in Trondheim and I went on writing it in Wertheberg, and then in London, and then on the *Queen Mary*, and then in New York, Atlanta, and finally, San Francisco."[In 1946, Paton was thinking of applying to be Director of prisons. As preparation, he went on tour to study penal institutions in Scandinavia, Britain, Canada and the U.S.A. It was at his own expense and took eight months.]

RH: "It's incredible that you have got that unity into it."

AP: "*Ja*, well, the other thing that I look back and find incredible was the fact that I could go out all day, in a strange country, catching trains and buses and going off to far-off places, and being shown around institutions—not the easiest way of spending your day, that I can tell you!"

RH: "Exhausting!"

AP: "*And* then come home at night and *want* to write—and *that*, I think, is what gave it the unity."

RH: "It is incredible, because all those impressions must have been there in your mind vividly, but yet you managed to push them out of the way."

AP: "Quite right, they were very vivid in my mind. It was my first visit to America."

RH: "Yes, that would be pretty enormous. Now, there have been quite a number of religious figures who seemed quite a big part in your life—Father Huddleston, and you in theirs, of course, Patterson…"

AP: "Which Patterson?"

RH: "John Patterson."

AP: "What do you know about him?"

RH: "Well, very little."

AP: "John Patterson was the Headmaster of Kent School, Connecticut. He brought great pressure on me to go and teach there for a year, which I refused. I told him that I couldn't go away. That was 1956, I think. The Liberal Party was just two years old then, and, therefore, I couldn't go. Eventually I went there for two months, and lived in the school, naturally, and took part in a very imposing—what would you call it?—not exactly a symposium but a series of lectures, Reinhold Niebuhr [famous German theologian], Jacque Maritain [French philosopher]... Who was that Jesuit?"

RH: "Modern day lecturer?"

AP: "Yes...Father..."

RH: "Is he alive?"

AP: "No, he died the other day. He was one of the most eminent of all the Jesuits. Father Courtney Murray was his name. To take part with these people was quite something, and then I kept very close to the Pattersons. They went to Rome, eventually, when he felt that he had done his stint at Kent, and he went and started an Anglican school in Rome, which we visited two years ago."

RH: "So he is still going strong?"

AP: "He had then retired, but the school was still going strong."

RH: "Are there any other religious figures?"

AP: "Michael—Michael Scott. Yes, Michael Scott plays a prominent part in my biography of [Archbishop] Clayton. Very fascinating, how Clayton wanted to see the Church active in the world. The people he found very hard to get along with were all the others who wanted to see it active in the world—a very fascinating enigma. And that is what I like about writing biography—you get hold of an enigma like that and you try and explore it as much as you can. He thought Michael Scott was unwise. He thought Huddleston was unwise. He thought Reeves was unwise. Those three, especially, because they didn't go about things the way that he would go about them. He was a great man, but... Huddleston pays a great tribute to Scott in *Nought For Your Comfort*, in which he says that he didn't really know what he was doing, and I feel ashamed now that I didn't support him more. I think that Michael Scott was one of the bravest, diffident men that the world has ever seen."

RH: "A marvellous tribute to him."

AP. "Yes, because he wasn't really cut out for that kind of thing."

RH. Yes, that makes it very tough. And Charles Hooper?

AP: "Charles Hooper, no—not a great man."

RH: "What about philosophical religious things which have influenced you, people who you've read?"

AP "Well, I'll speak to you from [George] Herbert [the C17th poet]..."

RH: "What about religious thinkers? Has Ghandi had an influence on you?"

AP: "I've been the Chairman of the Board of Trustees of the Phoenix Settlement for the last fifteen years, or so. I think that I would find that it would be going too far to say that Ghandi influenced me, because, you see, Ghandi's life was in a way very reminiscent of Christ's life. But I had a tremendous esteem for Gandhi. You see, people often say, "What writers influenced me?" But I quite frankly don't know. I don't think that any writer has influenced me."

RH: "No, I wasn't thinking influencing you in the sense of your style, but simply figures that bulk large in your mental life—religious figures at one period or another in your life."

AP: "Well, I would say I would certainly include Ghandi, and I would include [Abraham] Lincoln, and I would include Francis of Assisi—perhaps more than most."

RH: "You mentioned Jacques Maritain a short time ago—any philosophers of that kind?"

AP: "You know, that life is so short, and time is so little, that I can't afford to read philosophy, you see."

RH: "I know exactly what you mean."

AP: "I just can't afford it. I mean, there are hundreds of books one would like to read, and I just haven't got the time to read them. If I had to start reading, say, St Augustine, or Freud, or Bergson, or Whitehead, I have got to throw all these things [indicates his desk] off the table—work. And if you have done this kind of work for a good part of the day, then you don't want to do this work at night;

and I don't try to. That's why you're getting ahead tonight, because I like to sit down, and I don't smoke during the daytime. I only smoke at night when we have our drinks."

RH: "A pipe, do you smoke?"

AP: "No, cigarettes. Have our drinks, do a puzzle. Perhaps I might read again when I go to bed, but I don't try and do any serious reading in the evening. If there is a serious book that I must read, I'll make it part of my work, and I will read it during the daytime."

RH: "You were reading *The Washing of the Spears* [*The Washing Of The Spears: The Rise And Fall Of The Zulu Nation* by Donald R. Morris] the last time I was here."

AP: "Well now, that's the kind of book that you could read at odd times. It was exceptionally well written, but philosophy is very tough."

RH: "I know. Now, I wonder, Mr Paton, if you could give me more details of the founding of the Liberal Party. I wonder, for example, if you could tell me, as far as you can recollect, how the thing came about in the kind of personal details and people you met and how the idea grew. Just in as detailed a way as you can."

AP: "When I retired from Diepkloof Reformatory in the middle of 1948, my wife and I went to live at Anerley—Anerley [A small place on the south coast of Natal]. It was actually an idyllic life. You get up in the morning and you go and bathe, come back, and then have breakfast, and read your paper, and then you go to the Post Office and get the post, come back and you read your post and anything else. After lunch you have a siesta; and then at 4 o'clock you have tea, and you go for a walk. And then we all finished to go for another bathe in the evening, late afternoon. I thought I would never go back to… you know, I had thirteen years of Diepkloof Reformatory, of really hard work. And then I think both of us began to feel, really, that we were too far away from the world. Very nice to go down there when you are sixty or seventy, although, as a matter of fact, I wouldn't even now like to do it. We had a very good four and a half years. Then, in Cape Town, Johannesburg, Pretoria, 'Maritzburg, Durban, more and more people were coming together—the idea of starting some kind of Opposition very much in the air. No one thought of really calling it anything else but Liberal. The modern tendency to sneer at the word 'Liberal'—I don't take any notice of it at all. That's what I am, and that's how I'll die! In any case, the word 'Liberal' means so many different things, that simply to write it off—as many of our young radical people are doing today—but I don't have any sympathy with people who don't realise who their own mentors were. These young students, I mean... if it hadn't have been for the Marquards [Leo, b.1897 d. 1974, founder of the National Union of South African Students, historian, elected AP's co-vice-president of the Liberal Party in 1953] and the Hoernlés, they wouldn't have known what they are doing today. And so there was this growing feeling, and then Peter Brown asked me to come up to a meeting in Pietermaritzburg, at his house. And the same thoughts, very cautious, nothing spectacular, but simply a growing realisation that you couldn't sit down and do nothing—you had to do something. As I say, this was being felt in so many different parts of the country that we founded the Liberal Association. And as the Liberal Association began to get more and more impatient, we wanted to have a Liberal Party; and so a year later, in 1954,[4] we established the Liberal Party."[The Liberal Party survived for fifteen years but was terminated by the Political Interference Act of 1968. AP became chairman in 1956, and in 1958 national president.]

RH: "This was just really the two of you?"

AP: "Oh no no, oh no no, oh no, it was people like Wolheim and Marquard in Cape Town, and Unterhalter and Wentzel, and people

---

[4] It was, in fact, in 1953, as Colin Gardner has pointed out.

like that in Johannesburg, and Brown and his friends in Pietermaritzburg…"

RH: "It was an idea that was in the air?"

AP: "Oh, yes. Leo Kuper [Paton wrote the introduction to *Durban: A Study in Racial Ecology* by Kuper, Watts and Davies pubd. by Columbia University Press, 1958], people like that, in Durban; Jordan Ngubane [A man, whose intellectual abilities and moral character, AP thought highly of. Delegate to the All-Africa Accra Conference, former Vice-President of the Liberal Party, banned in 1963, author of *An African Explains Apartheid*, pubd. 1963 Frederick Praeger, New York.], Pat [Pumalengo], Selby Msimang [National Deputy Chairman of the Liberal Party about 1965, African academic, UBLS, Lesotho]. The sort of feeling that was going right through, and so that's how eventually the Liberal Party came to be established. And our first leader was Mrs Ballinger [Margaret, first elected by Africans to Parliament for 'Natives' in 1938, until the African representation was abolished under the Promotion of Bantu Self-Government Act of 1959, President of the Liberal Party 1953-1955, Chairman of the Cape Province branch in 1963, ex faculty member of Wits under the Principalship of Jan Hofmeyr], and then she felt that she wanted to have someone to do the other side—she would look after Parliament and so on, and I became the National Chairman. And then some of my friends came to me and said, when was I going to write this Hofmeyr [Biography?]. And I said, 'Well, I can't. I can't stay this big National Chairman of the Liberal Party and try and write a book.' So they said, 'You had better get off it.' And Peter Brown took on the National Chairmanship. They didn't want me to go unnoticed, so they created a Presidency—and I became the President. That's the story, more or less."

RH: "How did you set about funding the Liberal Party? That must have been quite a problem at that time?"

AP: "If I remember rightly, Peter Brown and I carried the main burden; nevertheless, we also had some very generous members as well. Our subscription was negligible. (I think it was 25 cents, or something like that.) When it came to a question of holding our Congress, then we would always help those of our members who weren't in the position to pay travelling expenses."

RH: "That must have been quite a burden for just the two of you to bear."

AP: "No, no, no, it didn't fall entirely on the two of us."

RH: "But largely—it could be quite a problem?"

AP: "Then you see, we didn't have to pay any salaries. Peter Brown was National Chairman and he spent a great deal of his own money, and there was never a question of paying his expenses, or anything; nor of mine, for that matter."

RH: "I was hoping that I would be able to see Peter Brown; but this visit I think it will be out of the question. It may be possible when I come back."

AP: "When you say, when you come back—when will you come back?"

RH: "I am expecting to be back in January."

AP: "I just heard—I thought it was the tail end of a conversation—whether you were thinking of leaving, going to England?"

RH: "No, no. I'm expecting to be back in January."

AP: "Was it your daughter?"

RH: "Yes, my two daughters are expecting to stay in Britain."

AP: "I see. How old are they?"

RH: "Seventeen and fifteen, the two eldest."

AP: "And they are going to stay with whom?"

RH: "Well they will go to school there. A-level college for Mia, the eldest, and Rachel will go to a Convent where she was before; and then my wife's mother is very close, at Berwick-on-Tweed, you see."

AP: "Now, righto what's next? Oh by the way, in 1960, Peter Brown was put into prison—the time after Sharpeville [1960]. So I took over the National Chairmanship for two months. I was presented with a book for that. I don't know what the book was. It described Peter Brown, or rather, he is not Peter Brown—he is largely incapable of paying an ordinary complement—but it is meant to be a compliment. What was the book?... No, no luck." [Note: during this exchange Mr Paton was rummaging through a bookshelf for the relevant book which he failed to find.]

RH: "Peter Brown is still under House Arrest, I suppose?"

AP: "No, he has never been under House Arrest."

RH: "Have I confused it with some other kind of restriction, then?"

AP: "He can't go to public meetings; he can't belong to any organisation; he can't go to a court; he can't go to a school; he can't go to a factory; he can't go into a dock area. Nothing that he says may be published; he may not publish anything; he may not attend any gathering."

RH: "What is the name for that kind of restriction?"

AP "They are all called Restrictions under the Suppression of Communism Act [1950]. House Arrest is still more drastic. You are ordered to be at home at six o'clock, and you can't leave your home until seven in the morning. Oh, and another condition is that you must report to the police once a week. There have been cases where you had to report every day. If you take a person like Helen Joseph [A prominent political activist], her restrictions were very severe. I think they were made intentionally severe, not to teach her a lesson, because they cant teach her a lesson."

RH: "But Peter Brown is still able to earn a living, is he?"

AP: "Oh yes. He has been running the firm of W.G Brown, in Pietermaritzburg. If my knowledge is correct, he no longer has a financial interest in the firm, but his brother and several partners run it. He wouldn't tell me this, but I would guess that this business really caters, very largely, for African and Indian wholesale buyers—probably shopkeepers, things like that. Well, the treatment they get in a place like that is such that they have had to leave the building and build a bigger one. Luckily, he has got that occupation; and then, also, they relaxed his Restrictions to enable him to visit his farms round about Mooiriver."

RH: "Now, something has puzzled me for quite a long time, and I haven't found a satisfactory answer to this. I wondered how it was that *he* is subject to these restrictions, yet you yourself, who had just as much part in the Liberal Party and just as active and so on, probably more so, the certainty is that you have escaped this kind of restriction?"

AP: "In the first place, I was not more active—I was rather less. The main responsibility fell on him, the work. I used to do a great deal of travelling and speaking, you see, but I didn't do the actual organizing. You may well ask the question. I think that I would perhaps give two answers to it. One was, that if the Government wanted at all costs to put a stop to that kind of activity, the only way that they could ever have got *him* to stop was to restrict him. That's the first thing. The second thing that I would say is—that my reputation with the [Education] Board may have hindered them from doing it."

RH: "Also, on account of the outcry internationally it would have made?"

AP: "Yes. Then, on the other hand, or even, while I tell you that, this Government is so irrational that one doesn't really know if any rational argument of that kind would appeal to them. They are quite capable of doing things that do antagonise the outside world."

RH: "They sure are."

AP: "So I can't tell you."

RH: "I thought, myself, that you were going to touch on something that had occurred to me. That he, being the titular organiser of the [Liberal] Party, they thought that if they struck *there*, perhaps a new organiser wouldn't be found, and that may have been the most effective way of stopping the Liberal Party."

AP "I would accept that as a third argument, yes. Even that argument would have to be qualified, because Dr G.M Naiker [Gangathura Naicker, a friend of the Patons, was sentenced to prison for contravening the conditions of his ban by inviting the Patons to dinner one evening] who held a corresponding position in the Indian Congress, also had these repeated bans, but he wasn't as active as Peter Brown. I think the fact both of them were titular heads is very likely true, you know: 'We'll teach a lesson to one of them'."

RH: "Now, the organ, *Contact*. Can you tell me how this came into being?"

AP: "*Contact* came into being, very largely, through the enthusiasm of Patrick Duncan [Son of the former Governor General of South Africa, member of the National Executive of the Liberal party, attended as a delegate the first All-African Peoples' Conference, Accra, in 1958, edited *Contact* for a while, imprisoned in 1960 for refusing to reveal his sources on Communism, flouted the conditions of his banning by opening a bookshop near Maseru, Lesotho]. I don't think Patrick Duncan was very wealthy—I think that probably his wife was."

RH: "He had a bookshop, didn't he?"

AP: "Yes, he did, and he appointed a retired chap called George Clay, and then, on grounds that most of us thought were quite insubstantial, he sacked him, and took over the editorship himself. We couldn't afford to have breaks in the [Liberal] Party at that time, so we swallowed this. Patrick embarrassed us more than once. He was a very unpredictable character. Don't think that I'm expressing any lack of admiration for him, because I didn't have any—any *lack* of admiration, that is. He was a very strong and brave character, but he was subject to these unpredictable decisions. We were subject to them too, of course."

RH: "Mr Paton, could we leave this topic, now."

AP: "I think that I ought to just say one thing more. When the party had to disband in 1968—because the Government made it illegal to operate a non-racial or multi-racial political organisation—we then established the magazine called *Reality*, which has been published ever since."

RH: "Yes, I subscribe to that. How active are you in that? You are Chairman, I know, of the Editorial Board, and you write in it. Do you take any part in the organising of the magazine?"

AP: "Oh, yes. We usually meet once a month. Every meeting we are planning for the next issue; it is a co-operative effort, but I am in the Chair. And then, in regards to the writing, most of the writing that I do for *Reality* is editorially, and that's anonymous by our custom."

RH: "Now, I was going to ask you about that. How much of the editorial writing *do* you do? Is it regularly, each issue?"

AP: "Yes, unless I am away."

RH: "I may have to ask you by letter about those, which editorials you didn't do."

AP: "Have you got all the copies?"

RH: "Well, unfortunately at one point the copies went astray; they didn't come to me. This was during my period in Greece [1970-1972]."

AP: "Well, I may be able to give you some."

RH: "Oh well, that would be marvellous! I don't have a full set—I have got *almost* a full set."

AP: "Do you know the ones that are missing?"

RH: "Not at the moment, I don't, but I could tell you when I get back home."

AP: "Well, write to my wife then, and if we are able to replace them, we will."

RH: "That's marvellous! I did write and ask, but I was told…"

AP: "Oh, but you are going on the 2nd July?"

RH: "Yes, but I mean, I could give you postage and so on, and perhaps you could send me two of them to Britain? There shouldn't be any difficulty about that, should there?"

AP: "Shouldn't be."

RH: "Well, I would be very grateful for that."

AP "In any case my wife is going to Britain herself at the end of July."

RH: "Oh well, that would be probably a way. Now, this is a question generally concerned with the way the choice of subject matter for your novels, and non-fictional pieces, has come into play—background effects, and so on. For example, I find there are lots of descriptions of natural beauty in your books. You describe mountains and seashores, the Karoo, Valley of a Thousand Hills, the Kruger National Park, and so on; but it seems to me that only one province, which in fact does not appear, and that's the Orange Free State."

AP: [AP laughs.] "That is true."

RH: "Now, I wondered why that was?"

AP: "I am just trying to think if that is *quite* true or not."

RH: "As far as I can search out, I can't find any references to the Orange Free State. But you would know better than I."

AP: "It is probably true; but I think that I must blame the Orange Free State for that and not me."

RH: "Is it a dislike of the terrain?"

AP: "Oh no, not at all. It's just that, Orange Free State, really—if you are an absolute, what's the word?—what is a chap with exquisite taste?"

RH: "Connoisseur?"

AP: "Yes, if you were a connoisseur of scenery, you probably can find something in the Free State. I know people who think that there is nothing like the Western Transvaal, you see, which is a very featureless country. But, really, when you have seen the Cape Province and Western Province—those mountains, and those valleys, and the sea. And when you have seen—well, that whole journey, really—from Cape Town right up the East Coast to the Eastern Transvaal. That—it's on this side of the Drakensburg, naturally, the most spectacular scenery is to be found—but I haven't got any animus against the Orange Free State at all."

RH: "It has grown on me, actually."

AP: "Well, I understand that. I am sure that if I lived in the Karoo it would grow on me; but I don't want to go and live there."

RH: "It isn't, in fact, connected with any kind of ideological dislike of the place?"

AP: "Oh, I don't think so. I would be very surprised if it were."

RH: "Another question about the locale. Is *Too Late the Phalarope* set in a real locale—is it based on a real *dorp*?"

AP: "Do you know the South Eastern Transvaal?"

RH: "No, not very well."

AP: "Well, it is based on that part of the country, the South-Eastern Transvaal, which is a grass country—which is a *very* Afrikaans countryside, extremely so. [AP pages through a Route Map.] The country up Ermelo, Standerton—well, not so much Standerton—Piet Retief, Amersfoort. I'll give you one more—Carolina, Breyten, Bethal—that country."

RH: "You know that country very well."

AP: "I've never lived there, but I have been through there many a time."

RH: "Yes, I've been through it. How did you choose it?"

AP: "Oh, I'll tell you why I chose it. I was once in Ermelo—no, Carolina—and my first wife, and the two boys, and myself, and a young Afrikaner from the Reformatory. And we camped on Carolina square, and after we'd had our food, I went for a walk;

and, as I was walking along, two African girls, running past, and then, to my astonishment, two Afrikaans-speaking soldiers, coming after them, with their heavy boots and all the rest of it. This was in the war-days, and there was a camp there. And I remember then thinking, 'I suppose these chaps had thrown away their restraints, and here they were in the army.' And I am sure that it is because of that, that I decided to put that part of the Transvaal in—because, if that had happened in days of peace, you can be pretty sure, too, that those two boys didn't come from that part of the world—they came from some other part, where they also felt liberated—you see? And that's the only reason that I can think of."

RH: "I see. I believe that originally it was based, was it not, on a newspaper cutting?"

AP: "Yes, that's true."

RH: "And I wondered whether the report had happened about that part of the world?"

AP: "Well, it *was* in that part of the world. [AP ruffles through the Route Map.] If I remember rightly, although it was a very long time ago, this thing happened in Nelspruit or Barberton. I remember the thing that moved me most about that story was that the fellow was a policeman, and that the wife sat in the court the whole time."

RH: "Now the style of *Too Late the Phalarope*—does it parallel fairly closely Afrikaans idioms and structures? Because I don't speak Afrikaans, but I would have said that there was certainly an idiom coming through which convinces me that it's an idiom of an Afrikaner thinking. Now, I wondered if this was a deliberate attempt, or whether it came spontaneously, or whether it was even true?—this observation."

AP: "Well, in the first place, it is no conscious attempt to do that. In the second place, the style of writing is quite different from the writing of *Cry, the Beloved Country*. In the third place, when you are writing about Afrikaners and an Afrikaans countryside, it's inevitable that their way of thinking, their idiom, should influence your writing; but I don't think that one does it consciously. Karl Kraus said there are two kinds of writers, the ones that *are*, and the ones that *are not*. With the ones that are, Content and Form are like Body and Soul. And with those who are not, Content and Form are like Body and Clothes."

RH: "Very good."

AP: "Which, I think, is *very* good indeed. So I said that seems to show, when the writer writes his book, that the writer must not be too cerebrally or clinically conscious of how he is *making* his book."

RH: "Did the style of *Too Late the Phalarope* come easily, or did you have to make several attempts before you got what you wrote."

AP: "Oh no, if I remember rightly, it came at once."

RH: "Yes, it's a pity you haven't got the manuscript, because I would have liked to have seen the opening chapter of that."

AP: "Yes, that would answer the question, wouldn't it?"

RH: "Yes. Another question, very like the one I asked you about the Orange Free State, but with a different slant. In your fictional writing I'm talking about you describe Afrikaners, and Afrikaner communities, and African societies and individuals and the English speaking Whites, and the Cape Coloureds. But I think I'm right, there isn't any description of the South African Indians or the Cape

Malays. Now, is there, again, a personal reason for this? I wondered whether, if you were, in fact, trying to give a comprehensive fictional picture of South African society, then perhaps you would have covered these two groups—but you don't. And I wondered if there was any reason for this?"

AP: "No, I'm sure there's not. If I were to write this third novel, which would be about the country as it is now, then that remark would probably not be valid. Except that, I don't really distinguish between the Cape Malays and the Cape Coloured people. When I would write about the Cape Coloured people I would be including [the Malay people]."

RH: "And the Indians?"

AP: "Did I never write it—even a short story about Indians?"

RH: "No."

AP: "No, I couldn't give you any reason for that. It's certainly not in the lack of interest, or anything of that kind. Because, as a matter of fact, in Natal, the people that one feels closest to is the Indian people—a person like myself."

RH: "So, I suppose, there is some reason why you haven't done it, but it is very difficult to explain?"

AP: "Might be that I didn't think that I was competent to do it, you see?—might easily be."

RH: "Well, it is obviously a difficult question to answer. Now, you have already answered this question this morning, but I wondered if, for the purposes of having it on tape for my records, you could tell me a little about it again: the way you came to be interested in, and the beginning of writing the biography of Roy Campbell. This was because W.H. Gardner had died and left the manuscripts, or was it a direct request?"

AP: "No, no, no. I had written, or given, a memorial lecture on Roy Campbell—which you have, or don't have?"

RH: "No, I don't have it, but I have seen it."

AP: "Right. I'll give you one, I think"

RH: "That would be marvellous."

AP: "It's in there." [Meaning, that the answer to RH's question will be found in the Roy Campbell lecture. Here AP takes a copy of the lecture from his drawer and hands it to RH.]

RH: "Thank you very much."

AP: "I'll explain to you about this. When I gave this lecture on Roy Campbell, I had read both his autobiographies [*i.e. Broken Record* and *Light on a Dark Horse*], and I had read his poetry. What I said in that lecture, which was given in 1957, sixteen years ago, is going to be substantially what the book will be; except, of course, for what new thing one learns; but the actual structure would be the same. Here, I don't want to make a claim – I think that one of the main interests throughout my whole life has been in the structure and mystery of personality, and I think that I've got a certain gift, which, if I hadn't had, I wouldn't never have gone to Diepkloof Reformatory. That one is able, just by small hints and indirections, to get some idea what the man is like behind the door, as it was with Hofmeyr. And, I think, I mentioned in *Hofmeyr,* one, or two, or three seminal remarks that he made to me in the course of his life, and *he* didn't know it."

RH: "Which gives you the clue."

AP: "*Ja*, he didn't know it. He was just opening the book that he kept closed so zealously. When he said that he stood on the same platform as Smuts, and he said to me, 'You know, Smuts isn't much taller than I am'—you see. Now, Smuts was probably three or four inches taller than him, Hofmeyr. It is a very odd thing to say. Another thing, too—when they [these remarks] slipped out, he said, 'If my mother died, I'd like to marry.' Which is more or less the same as saying, it is because my mother is alive that I can't get married. Or, what he said to Edgar Brookes. [Ex-Senator, friend of Jan Hofmeyr, joined the Liberal Party in 1962, became National Chairman in 1964, when Peter Brown was banned,] Brookes went to see him about something or another, and when they had finished off, Hoffie said to him, he said, 'I hear that your mother is not living with you any more.' Then he said, 'No, we decided the best, now, that she go and live by herself.' And Hoffie said, 'How did you manage it?' See? 'How did you manage it?' Which to me says a great deal—five words—and there was one more. You know, that when I first started on the book, Edgar Brookes wouldn't tell me that story."

RH: "Is that so? So he recognises the significance of it, too?"

AP: "Oh, he did, but he wouldn't tell it to me, because he thought that it might do harm. But when he read the book before it was published, he decided he wouldn't hold it back any more, because, after all, when one is trying to tell the whole truth about a man's life, why keep a part back?"

RH: "Do you think, as a biographer, Mr Paton, it is a disadvantage, or an advantage, to either have known, or not known, the person you are writing about? In the case of Campbell, I don't think that you did know him, whereas Hofmeyr—you knew him very well. Now, is it a barrier, or is it a help, either way?"

AP: "I met Campbell once. I describe, as a matter of fact, the meeting in the lecture; but, being what I am, I learnt a great deal about Campbell in those two or three hours. But, in any case, such a flamboyant, swashbuckling kind of character [AP points to a photograph of a painting of Campbell by his wife]—that you are absolutely fascinated by him, and you wonder what is actually being concealed. [AP displays two contrasting frontispieces of Roy Campbell.] These two pictures, by themselves, tell one a great deal about Campbell."

RH: "Oh yes, they are two different men, almost."

AP: "They are. This is the Campbell in the years when he couldn't write any more—when he was drinking too much. Mind, he always drank too much. He was drinking still more, then. It's my hunch that Campbell did not know what the extent of the damage he was going to do to himself, when he took the side of Franco in 1936. I think that if he had given you an honest answer, which he wouldn't have, he would have said, 'I have made a great mistake.' Because he alienated all his fellow writers—and if you are a writer, you don't want to be alienated from your fellow writers, do you?"

RH: "No, not a bit, or even from anybody, as a matter of fact."

AP: "Yes."

RH: "Was it [the painting of Campbell] by his wife?"

AP: "That's right. Yes—the swashbuckler."

RH: "Yes, that's him—but this is a chap I've never seen before." [Here the reference is to a later picture of Campbell.]

AP: "Very sad picture."

RH: "Very, very sad."

AP: "Very sad picture. And you know Mary [Campbell], I said to her, I said, 'Mary,' I said, 'do you know how sad a picture that is?' And she didn't. Very strange! Oh, she is very strange; she undoubtedly had a *very* great deal to do with his life—*very* great deal."

RH: "Now, have there been any of these, what can I say, 'keys,' or 'clues,' with these 'key' remarks in the case of Campbell that have opened the door suddenly?"

AP: "Oh yes, many."

RH: "Could you mention one or two, Mr Paton?"

AP: [Here AP reads an extract from Campbell's *Light on a Dark Horse*.]. 'Outside our lodgings, from Regent Square to the top floor of the Harlequin, at 50 Beak Street. Although we were very happy, my wife and I had some quarrels—since my ideas of marriage are old-fashioned about wifely obedience. And, in many ways, she regarded me as a mere child because of being hardly out of my teens. But any marriage in which a woman wears the pants is an unseemly farce. To shake up her illusions I hung her out of the fourth floor window of our room so that she [would] get some respect of me. This worked wonders for she gazed, head downwards, up at the stars. Until the police from their H.Q on the opposite side of Beak Street started to yell at me to pull her back. She had not uttered a single word and when I shouted out, pleasantly, across the street, 'We are only practising our act, aren't we kid?' She replied, 'Yes', as calmly and happily, as if we did it every ten minutes. The police then left us alone, saying, 'Well, don't practice so high up over other people's heads, please.

'My wife was very proud of me after I had hung her out of the window, and boasted of it to her girlfriends. This infuriated them, *as their young men always gave into them and they got no excitement or polarity. But it was five or six years before we broke each other into our complete satisfaction and I wore the pants for good. We both had such fiery temperaments that all our acquaintances had predicted a speedy and ruinous finish to our romance, which up to now has lasted thirty years.'*

RH: "Extraordinary."

AP: "Very extraordinary. See, I mean, in a way, for a biographer, it does pay to think about that for a day. What does it really mean? For one thing, I have met Mary Campbell, and Roy Campbell never wore the pants—I can tell you that."

RH: "Do you think that may be fiction, then?"

AP: "Absolutely true, absolutely true. But why tell it? Isn't that interesting?"

RH: "Very interesting. So it didn't happen as an event, even?"

AP: "She says it never happened. But she thinks it's funny. She just has no idea of what it means. It wouldn't surprise me—well, I'll tell you: when they came out to South Africa from 1924 to 1927 and went back in 1928, and Harold Nicholson and his wife, Lady Victoria Sackville-West, lent them a cottage."

RH: "Yes, I remember that. That's mentioned in the middle of the diaries of Nicholson."

AP: "Right, and it started off beautifully. And there was no doubt, whatever, that Mary and Victoria fell in love with each other, and they went off somewhere, and Roy cleared off to the South of France.' [Here AP reads from his own partly-written unpublished biography of Campbell. As a working title, he called his notebook *The Chronology*.]

'*Mary did not wish to speak about this episode. Mary's [altercations]—"We came near to separation. Roy Campbell was in a desperate state. He could earn no money. I don't want two accounts of the Sackville-West episode. He turned against the Sackville-Wests, because they were homosexuals. Vita was very fond of Roy and then turned to me. Roy's account of Vita is not true. She had in fact a sweet nature. After that we had a tremendous quarrel. Roy went off to the South of France in anger, but in the end, he begged*" [end of quote] *Mary to come.*'—I've written there—'*The truth goes much deeper than this, and this must be regarded as one of the most important periods of Roy Campbell's life.*'

[I think AP goes on reading from *The Chronology*, his working title for the notes of his MS on the projected biography of Roy Campbell.]

AP: " '*After the lesbian love affair with Victoria Sackville-West, she and Mary went off together. Roy was not only angry, he was in despair. He forgave Mary, but according to Rob Lyle, the scar remained forever. Mary became a Catholic; she went daily to mass to expiate for past sins.*' Quote: "*There had been a wild time in my life.*" End of quote. '*In answer to my questions*'—that's me [AP]—'*Mary said that she believed that when sins are forgiven, they are finished with. Why, then, the daily expiation? In spite of his pain, Roy's love must have been great*'—for see the dedication to Mary in '*Adamastor*'—'*the lapse was never repeated. But even at the age of seventy, Mary told me of men who would have taken her as a lover.*' That. to me, is very strange."

RH: "Very strange, indeed, incredibly strange. That's in your notebook, *The Chronology*, is it?"

AP: "*Ja*. You see, when people say, 'Well, why must you write the life of Roy Campbell?' I won't say that *anyone's* life would be worth writing; but I think that *his* life is worth writing, partly because he held these extraordinary ideas about Jews, and Pommies, and Quakers, and Charlie Chaplin; but yet at the same time, could write such poetry—because now, naturally, I would have to give a great discussion of his poetry, too; because, if you write in that violent and vivid—what did he call it?—'solar strain,' then you must be repetitive. You can't go on finding the violent words forever, so there is a certain repetitiveness. But when he writes—Do you know 'To a Pet Cobra'?"

RH: "Not well. I mean, I have read it, but I don't know it well."

AP: "Well, let me read you one stanza of it. Now, you see, this to my mind, is perfect poetry. I'm not using that word 'great.' I don't really know how one can distinguish between perfect poetry and great poetry; but I will read this to you. *This* is his 'To a Pet Cobra':

> With breath indrawn and every nerve alert,
> As at the brink of some profound abyss,
> I love on my bare arm, capricious flirt,
> To feel the chilly and incisive kiss
> Of your lithe tongue that forks its swift caress
> Between the folded slumber of your fangs,
> And half reveals the nacreous recess
> Where death upon those dainty hinges hangs.

You see!"

RH: "Yes, I had forgotten that it was so good."

AP: "Well, not one of the following stanzas is as good as that; but you see, if you can write 'The Serf,' 'Theology of Bongwi,' and 'The Zulu Girl,' and the first verse of this, and 'Tristan da Cunha,' and nothing else—"

RH: "He's written some fine poetry."

AP: *Ja*, that's true."

RH: "Yes. You touched on another question I was going to ask you later—when you raised it. I was going to say, do you think that he was a great poet?"

AP "You see, now, Roy became a Catholic. He writes about it in *Light on a Dark Horse*—the opening of a new life. Most extraordinary passage, really. This was into Languedoc and they weren't as yet confirmed by then—by the Cardinal.

'As on that day before dawn, began an entirely new chapter in our lives, which had hitherto been rather drab and dull compared to the new splendours of experience, for which we were lucky enough to be preserved.'

Well, now, I had to try and work out how deeply he meant that—and I suspect he *did*.

RH: "Yes, it is difficult to know, I suppose, on evidence, isn't it?"

AP: "Well, it is difficult to think how the chap who could talk like that—the same one who can talk so contemptuously of other people—very difficult."

RH: "You represent him, so far, as a set of contrarieties."

AP: "Oh, very much!"

RH: "Now, how have you managed to put them together?"

AP: "Just lend me that *Theoria* a minute! How about 'The Flaming Terrapin'? [Cambell's first published work, 1924, which brought him instant fame.]

'There is, I am sure, not much need for me to draw attention to Campbell's use of simile and metaphor; his use of colour and image; his use of words, both for their meanings and their sounds.'

This was not done to express deep ideas about the universe—he didn't have any. Campbell's fundamental and elemental idea was the universe itself.

Yeah, there is no doubt that he was fascinated by life and vigour, and banging—and he wanted his life to go out with a bang and not a whimper. I think he said so."

RH: "Yes, that is a quote from T. S. Eliot."

AP: "Oh, it comes from Eliot, and I think that Campbell used it before he died, for some time. I think in one of his books, as a matter of fact. Oh, as a matter of fact, just lend me that *Theoria* again—he actually wrote it."

RH: "Did he write it?"

AP: "To Mary—he wrote these lines:

> *You led me to the feet of Christ, who threatened me with lifted quirt and by its loving fury sliced I staggered upright from the dirt. And that is why I cannot simper nor sigh nor whine in my harangue, instead of ending with a whimper my life will finish with a bang.*

As indeed it did! At that price, you see, that although his life finished with a physical bang, I am afraid it didn't finish with any other kind of a bang; because, you see, another very interesting thing, to me, is that he should have turned to St. John of the Cross, in the last years of his life. I strongly suspect that he would have given a *great* deal to have been able to have written poetry like that. Whereas, his Christian poetry was poetry about banging, and so on. Christ was the cowboy, you see. Christ was the albatross."

RH: "Very interesting, that theory! I must say that gives him a new look in my eyes. I don't know Campbell anything as well as you do, but the image that comes out to me as being a swashbuckler, of course, is a very popular one. Even in his best poetry, there is the exhibitionistic."

AP: "Oh yes, well, you can't just hide it. [AP quotes Campbell's 'To the Sun']:

> Oh let your shining orb grow dim,
> Of Christ the mirror and the shield,
> That I may gaze through you to Him,
> See half the miracle revealed,
> And in your seven hues behold
> The Blue Man walking on the Sea;
> The Green, beneath the summer tree,
> Who called the children; then the Gold,
> With palms; the Orange, flaring bold
> With scourges; Purple in the garden
> (As Greco saw); and then the Red
> Torero (Him who took the toss
> And rode the black horns of the cross—
> But rose snow-silver from the dead!)

—You see, it was a magnificent poem, but he couldn't write: 'It was on a dark—' and what?"

RH: "I don't know it."

AP: "You don't know it? It is a very beautiful poem, and there is no doubt whatever, or there seems to be no doubt, that Campbell was the greatest translator of *St. John* [of the Cross]:

> Upon a gloomy night with all my cares to loving arbours thrust,
> Oh when cherub of delight, with nobody in sight
> I went abroad when all the house was hushed.
> In safety and disguise, in darkness up the secret stair I crept,
> Oh happy enterprise concealed from other eyes,
> When all my home at length in silence slept.

—He couldn't *write* poetry like that; he could *translate* it!"

RH: "Now, I think that the last time I was here, you mentioned that you were going to Spain to have a look at some of the places where Roy Campbell had been, and so on. This is obviously one way you have of getting under the skin of Roy Campbell for your biography. What other methods have you used?"

AP: "Well, there are those two pictures that I've shown you; these two books [of autobiography] that he wrote. My interviews with Mary. There is the story I told you about Sackville-West, and yet this extraordinary:

> Sweet sister through all earthly treasons true.

It wasn't true.

> My life has been the enemy of slumber,
> Bleak are the waves that lash it,
> But for you and your clear faith I am a locked lagoon,
> That circles with its jagged reef of thunder
> *The calm blue mirror of the stars and moon.*

RH: "Powerful."

AP: "*Ja*. He must have forgiven her [Mary, for the Vita incident] even though there was a scar left. He must have forgiven her. Well, that's a great thing! It also shows something else. It may also show that he couldn't afford not to forgive her."

RH: "You mean that he needed her?"

AP: "*Ja!* And he couldn't do without [her]. And so, you see, the more you think over these things, the more complicated and the more fascinating the story becomes."

RH: "I was wondering whether you had been able to look at things he used, things he had worn, things he had had around him, and whether these had given you any insights? This kind of thing?"

AP: "Well, I had spent quite a lot of time, but not in the house that he lived in, but in the house that he built. Very extraordinary house—very dark."

RH: "Is it?"

AP "*Ja*. Here was the man that brought 'solar colours' into verse. The house is dark—very dark house indeed."

RH: "Now why is that, I wonder? That's incredible."

AP: "I don't know. I think the happiest years of his life were on Martique, Camargue—that was the kind of life that he liked, you see. The other fascinating strand that runs through the book [*Light on a Dark Horse*] is that he had a father who really couldn't understand a son who didn't do any work—he couldn't understand it. He couldn't understand a son who just lay about and once a week,—once a fortnight—he would get a piece of paper and write something—you see? And this led to a great deal of friction, and it was the mother who always interceded."

RH: "Yes, now I am looking forward to reading this biography; it sounds fascinating."

AP: "Well, I am afraid all that has got to be done *first*!"

RH: "Do you have any idea how long it's going to take, now? Or perhaps it's not possible to put a deadline, as such." [AP eventually gave up writing it. He told me in 1973 that he was thinking of handing *all* his material to a young Oxford graduate who had shown an interest in taking it over. AP found Campbell's prejudices and beliefs difficult to accommodate in the writing of the biography. Finally, they became too much for him to swallow.]

AP: "Well, it's nothing like as difficult as *Hofmeyr*."

RH : "I believe you spent twelve years on that, didn't you?"

AP: "No, not really. It *took* eleven years, but then, for seven years, I did nothing. And then I *started* it—I probably worked for two years—and then the Old Lady [Hofmeyr's mother]—she made it very clear to me that she didn't like the way I was going, and she told me that her son had written the life of Monteyane in *one* year, and that he was only seventeen when he wrote it. And if she knew anything about books, she would realise that it was a boy of seventeen who wrote it. So then, I just put it away; and then opened the newspaper one evening to read that she'd died. And I realised that I had to start work; and I started work. At that time we would go down to the South Coast, Anerley, taking all the books with me. I would read for a week—maybe—and then I would start to write. The writing might very often take three weeks, so this was about a chapter a month. I used to get desperate, at times, because I had worked out how many chapters there were going to be—something like thirty-six or so. I would actually fall into despair. Here, I stood up before the world, and said that I was going to write the life of Hofmeyr, and at the end I was going to say 'I can't do it!'"

RH: "Well, it was a phenomenal task that you have done there."

AP: "And I don't mind telling you, writing the life of Clayton too, I have sat here sometimes and done absolutely nothing, and thought, 'Oh what a fool you are!', and I dare say I would have felt the same way about Campbell."

RH: "Yes; now, we haven't said anything about Clayton at all. Was this a self-imposed task? I don't want to call it a task, but you know what I mean; or was it, in any sense, a commissioned work?"

AP: "No."

RH: "Did you begin before you had any idea of publication?"

AP: "No. Wherever we used to meet Anglicans, in my generation, sooner or later, you'd start talking about Clayton. You couldn't help it. And, old Archbishop Paget, who was the Archbishop of Central Africa, said to me, 'Why don't you write his life?' And I said, 'No, it's too difficult.' Then he badgered me to do it. Then the Bishop of Zanzibar came down and said, 'Why don't you write this book?' I knew by this time so many stories... One has to watch, in a book like that, that one doesn't overload it with stories—anecdotes. But I mean, anecdotes are just... He was very much like Samuel Johnston—he couldn't open his mouth [without arousing public interest]."

RH: "So he is very memorable."

AP: "Yes—you see?"

RH: "Well, that *is* difficult. I couldn't get it right. I must say, the problem of selection must be enormous."

AP: "Well, I suppose I've used at least half of the stories, and I went on and realised that, if I went on and used any more, it would spoil it. For example, in the early years of his life, he was afraid of women; and then, as he became older and more—, well, he became a great figure in the Church And then he was elected Archbishop of Cape Town, and, I think, that his fear of women began to disappear. And he used to explain to his Chaplain Carter his reason for his lack of interest for women. His mother was *immersed* in good works. He was very fond of telling Carter the story of how he was about one day in his push cart with the maid, and a lady passed and said, 'Good morning, Geoffrey.' And when she was gone, Geoffrey turned to the maid, and said, 'Who's that?' And she said, 'That, Master Geoffrey, is your mother.' You see? And some woman said to him, 'Is it true, my lord, that you are a Woman-Hater?'—and Geoffrey had a great belly, you know, and when he laughed, this whole thing would shake—and he went off into one of these laughs of his, and he said, 'No, the trouble is I can't tell one from the other!'

One of the stories I like best—though it's not a true anecdote, it's more a descriptive story—is Geoffrey at Bishops' Court. He loved his clergy; here, they were sitting around the table, the tea was brought in, and a big plate of sandwiches. Old Geoffrey never thinks to hand out the sandwiches; he shoves his elbow in the sandwiches and talks away, you see. And then looks up and he sees all this mess, and he wipes it off, and he carries on talking, and back goes his elbow into the sandwiches again. That's also typical of him.

And, oh, people were terrified of him! They, with *few* exceptions, began to understand that he was a very holy man, although he had this very bad temper. He is quite capable—or he *was* capable on *one* occasion—in procession into the church, and the evangelist's wife, in great piety, had made a cushion, and put it right in the middle of the steps, and Geoffrey gets the cushion and kicks it aside."

RH: "Now this is a question connected with your biography, again, really. I believe that you started as a Methodist, is that correct?"

AP: "No. My people, you see—my father and mother—were Christadelphians; and when I went to university [the University of Natal] and became a member of a student-Christian organisation, and the idea of possessing 'that Truth,' or having a monopoly of 'The Truth,' became more and more ridiculous to me. My parents were very hurt when I wouldn't join them. I didn't become a Methodist, but I used to go to the Methodist church. As a matter of fact, I didn't become *anything* until I got married. My wife was an Anglican, and I was also much more attracted by Anglicanism than by any other, largely because I felt that, while it was concerned about Goodness, it didn't make quite so much a *fuss* about Sinfulness, and things, as some other people did. I mean, one knew that some of the holiest men were Anglican, you see? There is no doubt whatever that Christianity, by its preoccupation with *sin*, I think, did a lot of harm in the world."

RH: "Yes, I agree with you. Now this is one of the things which strikes me as being different, say, between your religious beliefs, as they are shown in your writings, as they come through, and somebody like T.S Eliot, who was also an Anglican—Eliot, in his great distaste and his preoccupation with sin, and especially with sexual sin. Now, there is none of this, any hint of this, in your own writings at all, an acceptance which seems to me to be complete and wholesome, and *whole*, about the physical side of life. Do you personally find Eliot's writing distasteful on this point?"

AP: "I can't say that, because I think that Eliot also understood the other things, you see. I would find it very distasteful, if I found a chap, who felt that being religious was to be against sin, as Calvin Coolidge is believed to have said. Do you know the story?"

RH: "No, but it rings a bell."

AP: "Well, he went to church and when he came back his wife said, 'Well Calvin, what was it like?' And he said 'It was all right'. 'What was the sermon like?' 'It was all right.' 'But what was it *about*, Calvin?' 'Well, it was about sin.' 'But what did the preacher *say*, Calvin?' 'He was against it.' And there is no doubt, whatever, that there was far too much of this. And I remember a chap, like David Evans [D.F. Evans, member of the Natal Provincial Committee of the Liberal Party, detained for ninety days under the General Laws Amendment Act of 1963, convicted of sabotage in 1964], who went to jail for five years or so—that's one of the things he said about my first wife. He said he, as a young person, felt that his nature was flawed, you see. He always liked talking to *her;* but he was never conscious of the flaws in his own nature; he was conscious of what one could do, what one could be, what one could aspire to. I find, too—exactly the same thing. That's why I liked old Francis of Assisi, because he too does not spend a lot of time talking about sins; although he called himself the greatest sinner in the whole world, mind you; but I think that is a form of boastfulness that applies to saints more than anybody else, maybe."

RH: "I asked you that question because I personally find Eliot difficult to swallow."

AP: "He is not my favourite poet."

RH: "His Anglicanism obtrudes; his distaste with the physical side of life obtrudes, although he is obviously fascinated by it all. And this kind of thing doesn't come through at all in your writing; and it seems to me, in a sense, to be what I would call two different strands of religious attitude and belief; it is the emphasis on sin rather—the retribution and punishment side of sin—whereas, the other is the acceptance of life as a whole—and the emphasis on the creative, and the aspect of love, rather. I wondered whether you, yourself, found it difficult to read a man like Eliot, because of (a) the temperamental thing, and (b) the religious emphasis?"

AP: "Well, I tell you, he is not my favourite poet, you see. I think that his faith was very real."

RH: "Yes, I am sure it was. But he was one of the 'dammers-up' of life, to me."

[There is an anomaly in the tape at this point. But I wanted him to talk about his poem 'Death of a Priest', written in 1970, about the Imam Haron, a Moslem leader arrested under the Terrorism Act, who died in mysterious circumstances in prison, September 1969. Some remarks are missing, but the discussion continues as follows.]

RH: "Could you tell me, Mr Paton, more specifically about the events that sparked it off. [*i.e.* the poem]?"

AP: "This chap was arrested by the Special Branch, and was detained one [hundred and] eighty days [under the Suppression of Communism Act], I suppose. And suddenly, the news came out that he was dead. The story was that he had fallen down the steps, and died; and there was an inquest. The magistrate, in a way, started deteriorating. The magistrate found that wounds could be attributed to this fall; but he did say that there were other bruises, and so on, which seemed too complicated to have been caused simply by a fall on the stairs. And there was a public outcry for an enquiry, which was never given. The Minister said that he was quite satisfied, and eventually the Government paid the widow R5000, or something like that. I just thought that I would like to write about it."

RH: "Now, the 'I' of the poem isn't the man who died, is it?—

    Most Honourable I knock at your door."

AP: "No, its me! I'm knocking at his door."

RH: "And the Most Honourable is the Judge?"

AP: "No, that's the Minister."

RH: "The Minister. Yes, I see."

AP: "Which huh—what shall I say? It's very ironic."

RH: "It is a very striking poem indeed, and a very moving poem. And that use of 'Most Honourable'—I wasn't sure that it was the minister, or…"

AP: "Well, it doesn't really matter; it's the chap at the top, there. As a matter of fact, it's rather like—I couldn't read a thing of Kafka while I was writing it."

RH: "Oh yes."

AP: "That idea that you would knock, and knock, and you would knock, and no-one would pay any attention."

RH: "Yes, very Kafka-esque, yes. Could you tell me again—I'm not sure that I got it down right—the exact title of your *Retief* novel which you began?" [Piet Retief, in Natal, was the suggested setting for his projected novel paralleling the life of Christ.]

AP: "I think that it was the *Death of Retief*—I especially made it an Afrikaner, you see. And this was a young teacher who left his job in the country, and came to Johannesburg, and then begins a series of very strange events. I can't think of how far I got with it now."

RH: "Yes, I am sorry that you haven't got it."

AP: "I don't think that I destroyed it. It must be somewhere."

RH: "What year? Can you remember what year you wrote that?"

AP: "Yes, I would think in the 'fifties. Let me think… When I wrote *Too Late the Phalarope* in 1952—Now, I wouldn't be at all surprised, as a matter of fact, if the beginning of the Liberal Party also interfered a great deal."

RH: "With that novel?"

AP: "I can't remember now—it was twenty years ago."

RH: "You can't remember exactly why you gave it up, then?"

AP: "I didn't give it up solely because of political activity. I gave it up because I became very dubious. I actually made a study of novels which dealt with that subject. Such as Jerome K. Jerome's *Third Floor Back.*" [*Passing of the Third Floor Back*, Hurst & Blackett, 1907.)

RH: "That is surprising!"

AP: "And Faulkner's… I can't remember what it was called now. The story of the war in France."

RH: "Not *Requiem For a Nun*…?" [The intended reference was, in fact, to William Faulkner's *As I Lay Dying*.]

AP: "No. Sinclair Lewis—what was *his* called? *Christ in Chicago*? But Sinclair Lewis, really—I mean, that was really a political novel. He was using Christ, you see, to narrow the window. But I don't think that he had any real feeling at all that it was a very poor book. And then, Melville."

RH: "Who? Melville? Herman Melville?"

AP: "Who wrote *Billy Bud*?"

RH: "Yes—Melville."

AP: "Yes, *Billy Bud*. And then Dostoevsky—*The Idiot*; you see. It is a very fascinating idea. You encounter a personality and realise that you are confronting 'somebody,' not somebody ordinary. I am trying to think, now. Well, Dostoevsky's story of *The Inquisitor* [*The Grand Inquisitor*], which is a very short one, of course—but also, I found it was a very moving story."

RH: "Now, when you say that you made a study of them, did you find that this helped you, or inhibited you?"

AP: "I came to the conclusion that it couldn't be done."

RH: "I see—that your idea couldn't be done?"

AP: "*Ja*—when I realised how other people had tried it, and it didn't come off—"

RH: "Would you say all those novels you've mentioned were in some ways failures, then?"

AP: "If *that* was the theme intended. A novelist could very well say, 'Well, that isn't what I meant at all. I am only writing an allegory, anyhow.'"

RH: "And there is no possibility of you taking that up again? You are certain that you have decided that it can't be done, and that you have discarded it for good?"

AP: "You see, I am not absolutely convinced that it can't be done; because, I am absolutely certain that, if Christ came to South Africa, he'd end up—well, he would end up somewhere—or whether he would be crucified, or something like that; but he would certainly go to Robben Island. He would break—*have* to break—many laws."

RH: "Yes, I am sorry that it [i.e. the MS of the projected novel] is not available. It sounds very interesting."

AP: "I will have one more look before you go."

RH: "Now, two specific questions. One about the man's gift of 'The Divided House'? I put it [The MS of the story. Earlier, he had handed me some to look at.] there, for you. At the bottom of page six, you have made one interpolation. It's in a different type of writing; your sloping looped writing of the earlier straight-rather-italic writing, and in black ink. So I guess it's been done much later. Now, can you remember how much later—for your writing to have changed quite noticeably?"

AP: "Well, I must point out to you that it wasn't writing—it was printing. It's printed—that's why it *looks* so different. My writing hasn't really changed that much."

RH: "I see; so it could be at the same time, roughly?"

AP: "Could've been. You see, I wrote many other stories, and didn't do anything with them. It was my first wife's insistence that I did something with them. So I fished them all out, and tried to get them ready for publication, and probably made that change—then."

RH: "Do you have any idea how long after the first writing it was?"

AP: "Yes, I have a fairly good idea. Anne [AP's second wife who was also his secretary] is always complaining that I won't put any date on them [i.e. on the MSS], and in a way, she is justified because... *That* is what my great complaint is against Campbell."

RH: "That he doesn't put dates on anything?"

AP: "Very irritating."

RH: "It *is* very difficult."

AP: "This was published in 1961... so I would guess that... 1961... I'll just check when I wrote 'King Kong'. [The musical play *King Kong* (1960), noted for Paton's score.]

RH: "Was *that* written about 1941?"

AP: "Oh no! Much later—*all* written in retrospect—those stories. I made that a matter of point... Trying to check when I wrote 'King Kong'... when....? Because that story, 'A Drink in the Passage,' was based on that."

RH: "And this one ['The Divided House'] was written about the same time as it?"

AP: "Yes, because I wrote a large number of reformatory stories. And I have an idea that I wrote them down angrily, and that would be 1952. Then, I didn't do anything with them. Eventually, my wife insisted that I did something with them, and they got published in 1961."

RH: "So it was a little before there, was it, that you probably made some of these alterations?"

AP: "I should think the alteration was made in 1959, when I got the thing ready for publication. Let' see, when was this published? This is published in 1961, also. As a matter of fact, I fear that I have been negligent in regard to the short story. I *could* have done more."

RH: "Have you got anything planned? You told me that you would like to do more, but I wondered if it had gone further than that—if you had anything in mind?"

AP: "Well, you see, my writing took a different course. I can't quite explain to you *why* it took a different course. As I was saying to you, yesterday, while writing a biography, while it solves certain of a writer's problems, it creates other ones, you see? The writing of *fiction* also creates certain problems, and solves other ones. If you really haven't got anything to write *about*, then you are much better to write biography than fiction."

RH: "But it sounds as though you *have*."

AP: "I have been doing a lot of writing these last few months. I worked up that review about *Na Die Geliefde Land* [Karel Schoeman's novel, published 1973]. I wrote a review about Shirley Cripps, to which I gave a great deal of time. I wrote a message for Helen Suzmann [From 1961 to 1974, she was the sole Progressive Party Member of Parliament], because they had compiled a book to give her. I wrote those articles for *The Tribune*—'Where Are You Going, Afrikaner?'—for when I turn seventy. I wrote that poem, 'Caprivi Lament.' I wrote a profile of Buthelezi. [Gatsha Buthelezi, Chief Minister of the former Bantustan or black homeland for Zulus in KwaZulu, 1976-1994.] I wrote that thing for [the University of] Yale.[5] I have done a great deal of writing. I suppose my preoccupation, at the moment, is—what's going to happen to this country? I often think, if I can open—just supposing there are a million pairs of eyes that ought to be opened in South Africa—if I open one pair every weekend, that is fifty a year. It would only take twenty thousand years to open a million eyes—and that's a job I've set myself. As a matter of fact, a young girl wrote to me, and she said she was sorry I had thought that I had wasted my life. So I said to her, 'I don't think that,' and I said, 'Come up and see me.' So she came up on Sunday, and I gave her the last chapter of Clayton to read; and so I asked her that same question. 'Wouldn't it have been better if he [Clayton] had never come to South Africa? What did he do? What did he achieve?' Maybe, if he had stayed in England, then he would have become Archbishop of Canterbury—that's certain! And if anyone had said to *him*, 'Why did you waste your life?' or 'Did you *waste* your life?'—it would depend on the person who asked it. One person might get a very sharp retort indeed. But, if some really earnest person asked it, I think he'd explain that, if you are a Christian, then that matter of wasting your life would never even arise."

RH: "Of course, *you* are a writer in which the roles of writer, as writer, and, let us say, teacher, are very close together; they are aspects of the same personality.

AP: "Yes."

RH: "And I think that you have the purpose of teaching in all your writing, fiction and non-fiction—it seems to me. Although I don't think that the teaching aspect in any way ruins your art—in your novels, or your short stories."

---

[5] Did he mean Harvard? In June 1971, he addressed the Associated Alumni on receiving an Honorary Doctorate.

AP: "Well, I'm glad to hear *that*, because I have very strong views about it. Well, you saw that a writer may have two purposes: he's got to have the *one* purpose, and that's to tell the *story*. He may have the *other* one, and that's to teach a *lesson*—but that must never obtrude."

RH: "No, the thing that occurs to me—in the case of, say, Bishop Clayton, or someone else—is to ask the question of whether he should have not come or lived his life differently. It's easier to answer than it is in your case, because you—as a writer of novels and poems and short stories—are, at the same time that you're writing, also opening eyes; but you are not opening them directly, as teacher; you are opening them, first as artist, and then by the representations of the life that you write about—the implications of looking at it in this way, then, does the teaching."

AP: "That is as it should be."

RH: "It is very much more difficult, I would have thought, to decide, therefore, where most of your efforts should come; because you are doing, in a sense, something *more* when you are writing novels and poems—than when you are writing, say, a biography, which might be historically accurate, enlightening and instructive. You are not making the same kind of artefact as you are with a novel."

AP: "No, but nevertheless I dispute your statement that the one teaches better than the other. I showed this Clayton book to Beyers Naudé [an outspoken minister of the Dutch Reformed Church and opponent of the South African Government]. Well, it has got a great deal about the Dutch Reformed Church in it. If Beyers Naudé says to me that you have gone too far, then I would listen; and I wouldn't listen to anyone else. He said that he wouldn't change a word. He said that he wants that book to come out so that he can use it with his young *predikants*. Because many of them just don't *understand* what this incompatibility between Catholicism and Calvinism is."

RH: "Is that so? Yes, I am not saying that that viewpoint is *my* viewpoint. But what I was implying, is that I can see why the young girl might have made that kind of comment. But I think that 'a man must do what he must do' as they say in the movies, and there it rests, really."

AP: "Yes, because when I turned seventy, I asked myself the same question. And all that you can say to yourself is that if I could live my life again, I would probably live it in the same way."

RH: "Yes, I can understand, also, the regret behind a remark like that—because you write such good novels, and stories which will live, and, therefore, the world wants more of them—people will want to read them."

AP: "Well, I'm going to England at the end of the month, and I come back middle of September, and the Clayton book is going to be launched on September 27th. I shall put it out of my life, except, of course, I will get letters. I am contemplating the possibility that I will go and see Mrs Campbell, and if I think that she is not going to live very long, then I might put Campbell aside for six months and try and write a novel. Because I also know that, you see, in writing these biographies, the novelist can write all the time. I have got a sense of the *dramatic* in life, you see. For example, one of the books that I used for Clayton was the *History of the Community of the Resurrection*, which is as dull as ditch water; just because the chap couldn't understand the *drama* that was playing—he just missed it completely."

RH: "Yes, this comes through in all that you write, but, I think, there is also another aspect to consider—that a novel is a more universal thing than a biography. It would reach many more readers. They would read a novel and they wouldn't pick up your biography on Clayton, or someone else—because they are not that kind of reader."

AP: "All right, that might be true, there is a counter argument, as well—that is, the kind of people who pick up your biography are the kind of people who are more likely to create a more just society—than the people who pick up your novel."

RH: "That's true, yes."

AP: "So now, I think, that one has to be very careful about exaggerating the influence of literature—the moral influence of literature. Now, I tell you, in regard to the question of boycott: if we get boycotted, in sport, in this country, I just couldn't care. If we get boycotted in literature or the theatre, I would care a little more. [In June 1963, forty-eight American & British playwrights prohibited the performance of their works in South Africa before audiences that were not multiracial.] But the boycott, which would worry me most, would be the boycott in education. If—who was it?—Isaiah Berlin, and Professor Ayer, got five-hundred academics in Britain to sign a pledge that they'd never come to South Africa—that would worry me much more than a playwright saying, 'You can't perform my plays.' I am not a great believer in the moral influence of the theatre, for example. And I don't think that that's derogatory of the theatre, but I don't think that that's necessary—surely one of the great things about the theatre is to—I don't like the word 'entertain'—but surely that *is* one of the supreme functions of the theatre?"

RH: "And literature?"

AP: "And literature, yes."

RH: "But, I suppose, the crucial test comes in the thing, when you consider a book—let us say like the Bible—which is a great teacher, and literature at the same time. The question arises that if it hadn't, in fact, been imaginatively written and conceived, would it have entered so many hearts?"

AP: "No, this is perfectly true."

RH: "Now, does this not apply, also, to a novel?"

AP: "Yes, but it applies equally well to a biography. If both the novel and the biography are badly written, then they won't teach anybody. And it is only when they are well-written that they *will* teach people."

RH: "Yes, but what I mean is, is not a novel, in a sense, more universal than a biography, because it's probably nearer to the kind of universality that is in the Bible? The imaginative, poetic dimensions of it do this—whereas it is very difficult to get this kind of dimension into a biography."

AP: "Would you compare the great prophets with novelists?"

RH: "Well, in certain ways, yes. I would compare them in the sense that they use many of the linguistic devices that a poet would use."

AP: "Well, they were *poets* all right—they were poets, all right. They were *great* poets, too. A very funny thing about Clayton—the language of the prophets *absolutely*—well, in as far as such a man could be enthralled—in as far as you could *say* of such a man that he *could* be enthralled—because he wasn't given to *being* enthralled. But *that* language! And he could read it with *such power*!"

RH: "He was a passionate man?"

AP: "I made the observation several times in the book, because, you know, when I am writing a biography, I like to keep on reminding people—I always have a...—the theme must surface, and then it submerges, and you don't see it again."

RH: "Like a dolphin?"

AP: "Yes. And then perhaps five or ten chapters later, it comes up again. And he [Clayton] had this extraordinary gift. He is one of the greatest readers that I ever heard, and he had no gestures whatsoever."

RH: "Bringing this out purely by his voice?"

AP: "No gestures whatsoever. You see, Churchill was a great actor. And, I suppose, Clayton must have been a great actor, too; but he would have been very suspicious if someone had said to him, 'Why do you act in the pulpit?' He probably would have been very angry, too. Time after time after time, people said, 'Did you ever hear him read *this*, did you ever hear him read *that*?' And, at the beginning of Synod, they would always have what I call 'the Sacred Synod'—a bit of a misnomer—but still! That was the Clergy—alone—at the first day of Synod, and Geoffrey used to open the Synod with a reading, which he'd choose himself—he was very fond of Amos—and the extraordinary thing was that both, in his reading and in his preaching, he had this very compelling effect upon people. I mean, there were gestures of the face. There were changes in the voice. But never would he use his hands. I have never seen him use his hands. Except, when he put his head in his hands after some speech which he thought was incredibly foolish, and he growled, it was very funny. However, return to the subject."

RH: "Yes, can we go back in time again? This is one question about the manuscript of a 'Life for A Life'—it is on the desk there. And, right at the top, you have written a small comment, which you scribbled out. It is about the events of the story."

AP: "I don't know. The only reason why they are scribbled out, I think, is because I didn't want the typist to type them."

RH: "I was wondering what those events [in the story] were?"

AP: "Well, they happened in Craddock. It happened in Craddock [A town in the Eastern Transvaal.]. A chap was taken from a farm by the police, for something that had gone missing, and the next thing he was dead. So his wife, well, his widow, went to the police station and demanded to see him. They said he was buried. And then she said that she wanted him *un-buried.* And they said, 'We can't do that; we can bury him, but we can't *un*-bury him. You will have to get an order from the Minister.'[Government Minister] And she went to the local lawyer, who must have been a very brave man, and *he* took up the case, and they couldn't get the body exhumed. That story is *based* on that."

RH: "Do you remember the year of that happening?"

AP: "Yes, 1959."

RH: "I wondered if it was '59. I thought it was."

AP: "That makes that story—that must have been the last one, you see."

RH: "1959 or '60?"

AP: "Well, it was published in '61."

RH: "So it must have been written in '59?"

AP: "'59. Probably was written in the same year that it happened."

RH: "Do you remember where you saw this report?"

AP: "Yes. It was in Tom Sutherland's newspaper, *Evening Post*, I think it's called. As a matter of fact, Tom Sutherland 'went to town' over it, determined to uncover it. So I wrote to him and said I'd like to write a story about this, and he sent me all the cuttings."

RH: "I see. Could you tell me, roughly, what kind of proportion of your stories come from newspaper cuttings? I've noticed that you've used them more than once."

AP: "You see—it's not so much a newspaper cutting, but some event that happens."

RH: "That is reported in the newspapers?"

AP: "Yes. They hold a Debutantes' Ball for Coloured Girls. The irony strikes me immediately—there they go, and they shake hands with the Administrator [of the Eastern Cape]—and if they were to go the next day to his house, they'd have to go in at the back door. So that's what made me write that. 'Ha'penny'—that was written about a little boy, who, I mean—he made up the story about his family—he didn't have a family. There was no Mrs Maarman who never came to see him, or anything like that. That is where you, sort of, develop the story with your own imagination. 'The Divided House'—yes—that boy—only in the actual case of Diepkloof Reformatory, there was not a sequel. The boy—after which we'd bought all the clothes, and sent him off to school—he just walked away and left everything. He couldn't go through with it. A 'Life for a Life'—that was from a newspaper story. 'Death of a Tsotsi'—I think that's pure imagination. 'The Worse Thing of His Life'—'The Waste Land' was based on an incident. 'A Drink in the Passage' was Todd Matshikiza. [Todd, who wrote *Chocolates for My Wife*, wrote the music for one of Paton's dramas,

Mkhumbane, a play for Africans.] 'Sponono' was a boy. What do you want to know about it?"

RH: "Well, it is a rather bare account and I wondered if you felt able to tell me, as far as you can remember, what happened?"

AP: "Well, it was published, also—I mean, it came out very fully. You see, what happened was, I spent the evening with some friends down here, and when I got to the Hillcrest Corner [on a main road to Durban, in Natal], these two young men asked me for a lift. I said that I was going to Kloof [where he lived at the time], and took them to Kloof; and then they said, wouldn't I take them to Clermont? [Clermont, virtually a suburb of Durban, some miles away from Kloof.] Because, they were afraid to go. At night, there are no buses; so I took them to Clermont. One was in front, and one was at the back. What happened next, I only remembered, perhaps, a day or two afterwards. I was sitting there with a hand around my throat, you see. And I passed out, and I must have pressed on the hooter, and a member of the Special Branch came to see what it was all about."

RH: "He happened to be about?"

AP: "No; but he happened to live near there—and he heard the hooter. And, he gave in his evidence—he said that as *he* came on the scene, this chap was just about to plunge a knife into me! And, that, as soon as he shouted, these two men ran away. When I came to myself, I was lying on the ground, outside the car. I had no recollection of it. Then the police came on the scene. I was taken to West Kloof police station. I had a very painful throat; but I didn't know why. As a matter of fact, I thought I had got a cold or something, laryngitis or something. And even the next day I didn't know. I sent for the doctor and told him that I had this very bad throat indeed. And I think that it was only the day after that I realised what had happened. Well, then, this fellow, this chap here, denied..."

RH: "David Ndlovo?"

AP: "Yes—denied that I had picked him up at all. He said that I had picked him up in Kloof, and that I asked him to go to Clermont, to see whether we could get some girls, or something. This story was told in the court six times—six times! I don't think that had anything to do with the magistrate. I think it was the Prosecutor."

RH: "By the same person, or by different people?"

AP: "They arrested a man and a woman, you see—and both of them told the *absolute* identical story. There was no doubt whatever, in my mind, that they were very carefully rehearsed beforehand. So that they could know the script and—"

RH: "By themselves?"

AP: "Yes, and I presume that from a legal point a view, a technical point of view, you are entitled to do this. But then my lawyers—they walked into the Court the next day, and they said, 'Who is being tried in this case?' Then Dick Cotton, Pat [Pumelingen?], an Indian lawyer, and at least one other—they came to the Court with the express purpose, the next day, of seeing—actually seeing—what was going on. And Pat, at one time, thought of writing an account of this very strange trial."

RH: "Very strange indeed."

AP "And the policeman gave evidence. He actually described the two men; and naturally—you know what gossips people are—they say—'Oh, well, what is going on here?' Well it lasted two days, I think; but I *could not* believe my ears when the story was told for the fifth and sixth time. The strange thing is that the fifth and sixth time it was told *unsworn*—an unsworn statement. Now, *why* should a statement be unsworn? *That* I don't understand. I don't understand enough about Court procedure to know whether you can put in an unsworn statement—you can repeat what has already been done before."

RH: "It was told by the same witnesses?"

AP "Yes."

RH: "Now, what occurred to me, do you think these men knew who you were?"

AP "No, I don't think so. Well, that's why the Special Branch came into it—because it was a political thing. The whole thing was so fortuitous that it couldn't have been."

RH: "Now, the thing that occurs to me about it is that, for this to happen to you, is one of the most ironic things that you could possibly imagine. With what you have done for Africans, and the interest of Coloured people, and so forth, and you of all people—that this could happen to you—is there not a short story there?

AP: "This nearly happened to me before, with three young white men, as a matter of fact. And the Prosecutor said, 'Will you perhaps be more careful, in future, in offering people lifts?' I said, 'I've no doubt I'll be more careful.'

It's been the practice of my lifetime to offer people lifts, and particularly Africans. Because, you know perfectly well that they won't get any transport; you see, that sort of thing. I would think twice before offering a person a lift, at night, but in the day time, I wouldn't worry at all."

RH: "When did this previous incident happen to you?"

AP: When we were living at Anerley—would be between 1948 and 1952. And we were at [Fauna] Beach. Three young men, carrying knapsacks, signalled for a lift, and we gave them a lift. I watched them in the rear view mirror, and I could see that there was trouble ahead. But, by that time, we were on a very lonely part of the road. Do you know that South Coast road at all?"

RH: "No, I don't."

AP: "Well, the road leaves the South Coast at Pennington, and it goes inland, and it goes down into [the] very steep [Intalooma] Valley. There is just nobody there at all. Just as we were about to go down the [Intalooma] Valley, I saw the chap in the middle sit forward. And so I went down that hill very fast; very dangerously fast. It was a very dangerous hill. And I think that he assumed that I would have to go down at 20-25 mph [miles per hour] and he would risk an accident. I must have gone down at about 40 or 50, and by great luck, at the bottom, there was a bus. I stayed behind the bus up to the top of the hill, where there was a hotel. Then I put the three young men off. I said, 'We're going down to the beach.' My wife said, 'Why did you do that?' I said, 'Because they were going to do something.' And she said, 'Well, I had a very strong feeling, too, that something was going to happen.' So then we went and had tea, at the beach, and we passed these three fellows on the way home. They were still going down to Port Shepstone. The next day they tried to rob the bank in Port Shepstone, and they all got caught."

FICTION AND HISTORY[6]

Fact and Invention in Alan Paton's novel
Cry, the Beloved Country

R. W. H. HOLLAND

In the author's note at the front of the novel appear the following words:

> Various persons are mentioned, not by name, but as the holders of this or that position. In no case is reference intended to any actual holder of any of these positions. Nor in any related event is reference intended to any actual event; except that the accounts of the boycott of the buses, the erection of Shanty Town, the finding of gold at Odendaalsrust, and the miners' strike, are a compound of truth and fiction. In these respects therefore the story is not true, but considered as a social record it is plain and simple truth.[7]

These statements are not as direct and guileless as they may seem. Indeed, they are decidedly artful. The events referred to are documented historically, but the writer tells us that fictional elements are combined with them in some way. How? As will be seen, the answer is not simple. And how exactly can a 'story that is not true' be

---

[6] An article by Roy Holland that was originally published in *Zambezia* (1977), 5 (ii), the journal of the Department of English at the then University of Rhodesia.

[7] Alan Paton, 'Author's note' to *Cry, the Beloved Country: A Story of Comfort in Desolation* (Harmondsworth, Penguin, 1960), 5.

considered as 'a social record' that is 'true'? This may look like a contradiction. But when one realizes that the term 'true' is being used with two totally different meanings the contradiction is resolved.

Any invented story is untrue in the sense that it has never happened and never likely to; although, if it ever did, the writer, persuades us that this is the way it would happen. Paton's first use of 'true' clearly means this. His use of 'truth' for the social record is a little more complex.

How can an account compounded of actual and invented elements be true? It cannot clearly be literal truth. Does he mean that the described events are true to the 'spirit' of things, although departing from the facts in some respects? The spirit of anything is open to interpretation and argument. His simple truth is not as simple as it sounds. If *Cry, the Beloved Country* is to be seen as both a social and fictional record, one does not have to read far into the novel to spot that there is an ambiguity somewhere in the chronology of events. It is worth looking closely at Paton's 'plain and simple truth' to find out exactly what it is and to see how he exploits the ambiguity of time-scales for his 'record'.

Events that occur within the time-span established by the invented narrative will be referred to as happening in fictional time; events that have actually occurred, and incorporated into the novel, as happening in historical time. Within the novel, fictional time will be seen to be given preference over historical time.

No author can invent a date in the way that he can invent an incident; unlike a character, it either has occurred or will occur. In a novel, a date acquires an ambiguous status. *Cry, the Beloved Country* is set in the year 1946. What does this claim amount to? Is the date merely a device to give an appearance of historicity to a record that has never happened? Or are real events being dressed up to look like some kind of invention? Is the novel perhaps trying to do both? Do we place the date, then, in fictional or historical time, or in both? The following discussion will try to show that it is best regarded as fictional, 'occurring' within the narrative, rather than at a specific point in history; and, will try to throw light on the questions about truth.

> At 1.30 p.m. today Mr. Arthur Jarvis, of Plantation Road, Parkwold, was shot dead in his house by an intruder...[9]

A precise time is first emphasized in Book I, Chapter XI:[8]

This is offered to the reader as part of a newspaper report; one of the characters, Fr Vincent, brings it to the attention of Stephen Kumalo by reading it aloud to him. There is no ambiguity about the given hour and there is no necessity for it to occur historically—until a day and a date are assigned to it. It is not only fictional, but also essentially timeless, because 1.30 p.m. could, within the book, occur last year, this year, sometime, never. Any one moment is as credible as any other.

However, this particular event of the shooting of Arthur Jarvis is not left timeless. In court, at the trial of Absalom and his friends:

> A white man stands up and says that these three are accused of the murder of Arthur Trevelyan Jarvis, in his house at Plantation Road, Parkwold, Johannesburg, on Tuesday the eighth day of October, 1946, in the early afternoon.[10]

Now the instant of the murder has become actual; a fictional specificness has become an actual specificness. Also it has been linked to a particular place. But when a writer is so precise about the timing of a single incident in a story, he is not necessarily wanting the reader to believe that he is describing a factual event. The happening could be

---

[8] Apart, that is, from the date on the letter to Stephen Kumalo sent by Msimangu (25 September 1946) which starts off the entire action of the novel, *Cry, the Beloved Country*, Bk I, ch. ii, 10.

[9] Ibid., Bk I, ch. xi, 65.

[10] Ibid., Bk II, ch. v,137.

imaginary, but the timing real. He may wish the reader to understand that an action could have occurred at a precise point in history, and that the reader could have experienced it. Such a blending of the invented and the real gives more convincingness to his story. In such instances, reality and fantasy do not conflict.

But if, for example, a character is described as going to the police with information about a murder that has just happened on the day before the murder occurs, we sit up incredulously. A mistake of this kind—an incongruity in fictional time—would destroy the artistic illusion, and writers take care not to make this kind of error. So, giving a real date and time for any fictional event need not throw up any problem of ambiguous chronology, as long as the invented incidents do not conflict with it. We are thus able to think of Arthur Jarvis's murder as happening in fictional and historical time simultaneously, thereby giving convincingness to an imaginary happening.

But a puzzling ambiguity can occur if a writer does the opposite; that is, introduce into an imaginary account events that are recorded historically. Real calendars and maps are then superimposed on the mock world of the fiction. Alice can live in the day-to-day world, with its formal logic, its measurable space and its regular tick. Or she can walk through the glass and live in the other, with its zany logic, its unpredictable space and its reversible time. Only when one is forced into the order of the other might a breakdown occur.

Yet it is clear from the 'Author's Note' that Paton has fused history and fiction. What consequences does this have for the temporal structure of the novel? In giving his evidence, Absalom (the murderer of Arthur Jarvis and son of Stephen Kumalo) claims that, after the killing, he walked among the Alexandra Bus Boycotters:

> —And on the second day you walked again to Johannesburg?
> —Yes.
> —And you again walked amongst the people who were boycotting the buses?

—Yes.

—Were they still talking about the murder?

—They were still talking. Some said they heard it would soon be discovered.

—And then?

—I was afraid.[11]

This places Absalom, an imaginary character who has committed a murder at 1.30 p.m. in fictional time, firmly into historical time. Because the Alexandra Bus Boycott is a documented fact, the imaginary crime has been thrust into the context of history. Flesh and blood boycotters have even talked about the fictional crime, it is claimed. Obviously, merely to accept this much, the reader needs Coleridge's 'willing suspension of disbelief for the moment which constitutes poetic faith'. Of course, readers willingly give it. However, Paton's claim that his book 'considered as a social record...is the plain and simple truth' prompts the critical reader to compare the novel's account with the historical record. This is where the trouble begins.

The Alexandra Bus Boycott began on 14 November 1944[12] and lasted for seven weeks.[13] Absalom's crime is committed on 8 October 1946. The fictional and historical clocks are striking at different times. Paton has distorted actual chronology for the sake of his story by placing the boycott two years after its time.

There was, it is true, more than one Alexandra Bus Boycott.[14] Could Paton be thinking of the other one? Possible, but unlikely, for two reasons. First, it happened even earlier—in August 1943—and lasted nine days. This would require a delay of three years to fit the novel's

---

[11] Ibid., Bk II, ch. v, 143.

[12] The dates in E. Callan, *Alan Paton* (New York, Twayne, 1968), 50, 52, appear to be erroneous.

[13] See E. Roux, *Time Longer than Rope: A History of the Black Man's Struggle for Freedom in South Africa* (Madison, Univ. of Wisconsin Press, 1966), 318-19.

[14] '...twice during the war the workers of Alexandra had defeated the attempts of a bus company to raise fares by walking the twenty miles to and from work each day...', E. A. Walker, *A History of Southern Africa* (London, Longman, 3rd ed., 1957), 756-7.

chronology, making Paton's account of contemporary problems (he wrote the novel in 1947) less contemporary than need be. Second, the evidence of the novel itself suggests fairly conclusively that it is the boycott of 1944 he is thinking of.

Alexandra was an African location to the south west of Johannesburg within the jurisdiction of the Johannesburg City Council; and Paton also wrote a factual account of it (in addition to the one in the novel) twenty-six years after the writing of *Cry, the Beloved Country*. For the historical record, Paton has had to check his facts; for the fiction, he need not have done so. Nevertheless, that the novel is based firmly on factual details here is one of the conclusions that emerges from the comparison:

> African wages were so low that a rise of a penny in any staple commodity was a blow to struggling people. The bus fare from Alexandra Township to the city was raised by just that amount, and the workers of Alexandra, men and women, old men and old women, physical weaklings and cripples, refused to use the buses and walked to and from the city, twenty or twenty-two miles a day. Those who started work at 7 a.m. would have to rise at 3 a.m. and start walking at 4 a.m. If they finished work at 5 p.m. they would get home by 8 p.m. A great part of the distance was the length of Louis Botha Avenue, lined with comfortable white houses, whose occupants had of necessity to watch the daily march. Some white people were deeply moved by the marching protest, and would come daily with their cars to help the old and crippled, often being warned by the police that they were breaking the law. Others were angered by it and thought it should be ended by force. It is a temptation of white authority to this very day to silence black protest by force. Most of the white people of Johannesburg had no conception of the importance of twopence per day to most African people.[15]

---

[15] Alan Paton, *Apartheid and the Archbishop: The Life and Times of Geoffrey Clayton, Archbishop of Cape Town* (Cape Town, Philip, 1973), 143.

Fiction and History

The novel's account appears in Book I, Chapter VIII, where Paton makes the old African pastor, Stephen Kumalo (distressed and poor, seeking his lost son Absalom in the squalid locations around Johannesburg) face a walk of eleven miles into Alexandra, and another walk out again of the same distance. In fictional chronology, it happens on 7 October 1946. The similarities of detail in the two accounts will be apparent. The novel reads as follows:

> ...But here they met an unexpected obstacle, for a man came up to them and said to Msimangu, Are you going to Alexandra, umfundisi?
>
> — Yes, my friend.
>
> — We are here to stop you, umfundisi. Not by force, you see—he pointed—the police are there to prevent that. But by persuasion. If you use this bus you are weakening the cause of the black people. We have determined not to use these buses until the fare is brought back again to fourpence.
>
> — Yes, indeed, I have heard of it.
>
> He turned to Kumalo.
>
> — I was very foolish, my friend. I had forgotten that there were no buses; at least I had forgotten the boycott of the buses.
>
> — Our business is very urgent, said Kumalo humbly.
>
> — This boycott is also urgent, said the man politely. They want us to pay sixpence, that is one shilling a day. Six shillings a week, and some of us get thirty-five or forty shillings.
>
> — Is it far to walk? asked Kumalo.
>
> — It is a long way, umfundisi. Eleven miles.
>
> — That is a long way, for an old man.
>
> — Men as old as you are doing it every day, umfundisi. And women, and some that are sick, and some crippled, and children. They start walking at four in the morning, and they do not get back till eight at night. They have a bite of food, and their eyes hardly close on the pillow before they must stand up again, sometimes to start off with nothing but hot water in their

stomachs. I cannot stop you taking a bus, umfundisi, but this is a cause to fight for. If we lose it, then they will have to pay more in Sophiatown and Claremont and Kliptowri and Pimville.

— I understand you well. We shall not use the bus.

The man thanked them and went to another would-be traveller.

— That man has a silver tongue, said Kumalo.

— That is the famous Dubula, said Msimangu quietly. A friend of your brother John.[16]

The aged, the crippled and the sick are referred to in both; the times given to cover the distance correspond exactly; and the distance itself tallies.[17] Furthermore, references to the lifts offered to Africans by Whites, and references to Louis Botha Avenue, appear in both. Here is the novel again:

So they walked many miles through the European City, up Twist Street to the Clarendon Circle, and down Louis Botha towards Orange Grove. And the cars and lorries never ceased, going one way or the other. After a long time a car stopped and a white man spoke to them.

— Where are you two going? he asked.

— To Alexandra, sir, said Msimangu, talking off his hat.

— I thought you might be. Climb in.[18]

The similarities in the two accounts clearly help to enforce the conclusion that it is the second Alexandra Bus Boycott, of November 1944, that Paton is writing about in the novel.

---

[16] *Cry the Beloved Country*, Bk I, ch. viii, 39-40.

[17] I suspect that the reason Paton says 'twenty or twenty-two' in the first and not simply 'twenty-two' as he does in the novel is that he used Walker's *History* when he came to write the later account. Walker appears frequently in the bibliography to *Apartheid and the Archbishop*.

[18] *Cry, the Beloved Country*, Bk I, ch. viii, 41.

Fiction and History

There is a further piece of evidence to support the view. The first boycott was a totally spontaneous affair and lasted only nine days. The second boycott was quite a different kettle of fish. The first owed almost 'nothing to political leadership',[19] the second owed everything to it. An 'emergency committee' was set up (the main reason the Africans held out for seven weeks) and according to Roux, '...The leading figure on the committee was Gaur Radebe, himself a resident of the township'[20] Gaur Radebe may indeed be a possible prototype for Dubula of the silver tongue.

There was a third Alexandra Bus Boycott; but as that did not take place until March 1957, it can be clearly ruled out. It seems reasonable to conclude that the boycott intended in *Cry, the Beloved Country* is that which began on 14 November 1944.

To return to the matter of fictional and historical time. As there is a discrepancy of two years between the real boycott and the fictional walk of Absalom, the question arises: How shall the incident be regarded? They cannot be simultaneous events. Fictional time has to be regarded as predominant, because it measures the dimension in which the imaginary events of the novel occur and in which the invented characters act out their lives; and it is measured consistently. Thus, the proposal made earlier: it is best to regard the date of the murder, 8 October 1946, as a purely fictional date and not a historical one, as the reader inclines to do at first. The clock of the novel provides the Greenwich Mean Time, and the clocks of history must be made to agree with it.

The foregoing analysis illustrates a technique that is characteristic of the entire novel. Paton uses it first in Book I, Chapter VIII, with the incident discussed above. He uses it almost immediately again in Chapter IX. On occasion its use is even more noteworthy. An examination of the second instance tells a lot about the structuring of

---

[19] Roux, *Time Longer than Rope*, 319.

[20] Ibid.

the novel, the intention of its author, his beliefs, and the meaning of the work.

Chapter IX is the first of the remarkable choric sections of the book.[21] They are dramatic and lyrical and poetic in a way that helps to give the novel its distinctive flavour and style. Let us consider the temporal function of the section and how it fits into the two chronologies.

The marker of Paton's choric sections is the use he makes of the present tense. He writes in what may be termed the present historic. In English, narrative is normally marked by the use of the past historic in the third person. Indeed, Paton himself uses it orthodoxly for his own purely narrative sections (for example, Book I, Chapter V). The 'tension' that Paton sets up between the narrative sections (in the past tense) and the choric sections (in the. present) helps to give urgency, width of reference and social relevance to *Cry, the Beloved Country*. Chapter IX begins thus:

> All roads lead to Johannesburg. If you are white or if you are black they lead to Johannesburg. If the crops fail, there is work in Johannesburg. If there are taxes to be paid, there is work in Johannesburg. If the farm is too small to be divided further, some must go to Johannesburg. If there is a child to be born that must be delivered in secret, it can be delivered in Johannesburg.[22]

The sense that this is happening now implies also that it will continue. Not only do all roads lead at the moment to Johannesburg, they will do so in the future, as they have done in the past. Social problems are thus given a property of timelessness, illustrative of the eternal human situation and eternal dilemmas. This effect is part of what Paton wants, and may be termed the aftermath, or future, function of the present tense.

---

[21] Other 'choric' examples occur in Bk I, ch. ii, xii; and Bk II, ch. v, vi and ix.

[22] Ibid., Bk I, ch. ix, 48.

So, together with this 'aftermath' function, the illusion is kept up that the events are also happening right now. Often, the 'nowness' of the present tense is emphasized by small linguistic changes that suppress or play down the 'aftermath' function. By the use of a simple demonstrative 'this', for example, the 'nowness' of the night is brought vividly out and the 'aftermath' effect diminished:

> This night they are busy in Orlando.

Again, the insertion of 'tonight' has the same effect:

> Let us go tonight and cut a few poles quietly.[23]

Now, we are in the middle of the African slum building itself around us, witnessing the actual process of the erection, subtly made part of it and partly responsible for it.

> This night they are busy in Orlando. At one house after another the lights are burning. I shall carry the iron and you my wife the child, and you my son two poles, and you small one, bring as many sacks as you are able, down to the land by the railway lines. Many people are moving there, you can hear the sound of digging hammering already. It is good that the night is warm, and there is no rain. Thank you, Mr. Dubula, we are satisfied with this piece of ground. Thank you, Mr. Dubula, here is our shilling for the committee.
>
> Shanty Town is up overnight. What a surprise for the people when they wake in the morning. Smoke comes up through the sacks, and one or two have a chimney already. There was a nice chimney-pipe lying there at Kliptown Police Station, but I was not such a fool as to take it.

---

[23] Ibid., 52.

> Shanty Town is up overnight. And the newspapers are full of us. Great big words and pictures. See, that is my husband standing by the house. Alas, I was too late for the picture. Squatters, they call us. We are the squatters. This great village of sack and plank and iron, with no rent to pay, only a shilling to the Committee.
>
> Shanty Town is up overnight. The child coughs badly, and her brow is hot as fire. I was afraid to move her, but it was the night for the moving. The cold wind comes through the sacks. What shall we do in the rain, in the winter? Quietly my child, your mother is by you. Quietly my child, do not cough any more, your mother is by you.[24]

Each separate cameo (enclosed between asterisks in this chapter) is a part of the Africans' general plight, as well as episodes in the account of the building of Shanty Town; we are made to realize that the general points to the particular; all is tending towards the focal point of this particular night. Although earlier the reader was persuaded to accept the situations as timeless, and the comments as those made by the author on an eternal human predicament, he is now made to accept it as an immediately urgent dilemma of one particular night, 7 October 1946, an event of weight and importance in the chronology of the novel. Paton has it both ways: both timeless and timeful. The events happen on his fictional clock, and on no clock at all, for the eternal is timeless.

Roux's account of the historical Shanty Town runs as follows:

> The war [i.e. 1939-45] industries had drawn large numbers of African workers into the urban areas. Since Native housing schemes automatically came to an end in 1940, the resulting congestion in the urban locations can be imagined. On the Witwatersrand there were literally thousands of people without homes. Things came to a head at Orlando in April, 1944. The location had become supersaturated with human beings; it

---

[24] Ibid., 52-3.

could no longer hold all those who were trying to live there. Some thousands of men, women and children left the location and camped on vacant municipal ground nearby. They built themselves shelters of sticks, sacking, old tins, and maize stalks. Thousands of other homeless persons came to join them from other parts of the Reef. Thus was Shanty Town born.[25]

The difference between the two purposes is clear: Roux is out to record the social and historical fact that Shanty Town was built. Paton wants to show Shanty Town in a process of becoming; a variety of aspects emerge, but it is not seen as a sociological phenomenon primarily. Human drama and personal hardship are foregrounded by using the persona of Mrs Seme, an African wife and mother. She seeks lodgings with an Orlando family but is turned away. She hears 'the uncrowned king of Shanty Town' (in real life, Sofazonke Mpanza)[26] propose the building of their shelters:

—And where do we put the houses?

—On the open ground by the railway line, Dubula[27] says.

—And of what do we build the houses?

—Anything you can find. Sacks and planks and grass from the veld and poles from the plantations.

—And when it rains.

—Siyafa. Then we die.[28]

Mrs Seme goes to see an African official of the Johannesburg Housing Committee. He turns out to be corrupt and asks for five pounds.

---

[25] Roux, *Time Longer than Rope*, 322-3.

[26] Ibid., 323.

[27] It is worth noting that, in the novel, Dubula organizes both the Bus Boycott and the building of Shanty Town. In fact, they were two different men—Gaar Radebe and Sofazonke Mpanza respectively. Another example of artistic distortion.

[28] *Cry, the Beloved Country*, Bk I, ch. ix, 50.

The whole sequence illustrates the way Paton can bring out the 'aftermath' function of the present, as well as its 'nowness'. In a section that is primarily choric and static, he is nevertheless able to suggest a narrative by exploiting the temporal ambiguity of the tense. From the point of view of fictional and historical time, however, what is important to notice is that Shanty Town is firmly fixed in history in April 1944, whereas, fictionally, it happens on the night of 7-8 October 1946. Paton has again distorted historical time in the interests of fiction by an amount of two years. In fact, the Bus Boycott and Shanty Town were seven months apart. In the novel, this is compressed into about twenty hours. This is the second distortion of time for the sake of the fiction.

Finally, there is another and possibly more revealing discrepancy. The month of the Bus Boycott was November; Shanty Town thus happened first. In the novel, Paton reverses this sequence: Shanty Town follows the boycott.

One of his aims is clear from the extracts given: he wishes the physical upheaval, social suffering and individual misery depicted in the Shanty Town[29] episode to be placed alongside a climactic fictional event—the murdering of Arthur Jarvis by Absalom and all its consequent misery. The two events are thus associated in our minds. This deliberate juxtaposition—the real against the fictional—is fruitful in suggesting that the two are causally related, that the murder of a white man (who, ironically, happens to be active on behalf of Africans) by an unknown Zulu drifting rootlessly about the African locations around Johannesburg has been directly caused by the society that produced Shanty Town. Paton does indeed believe that African crime can be largely attributed to the conditions in which Africans are

---

[29] There were other 'shanty town' incidents that occurred in 1946 at Pimville and Albertynsville, which were recent in Paton's memory when he wrote Cry, *the Beloved Country* in 1947. Roux says that over '25 000 Africans have built themselves shanty towns of some thousands of huts roughly made of hessian stretched over a framework of split poles', *Time Longer than Rope,* 324. These events could account only for some of the details of materials used in the novel's descriptions, such as hessian. But Shanty Town itself was the proper name of one place. The others had different names. Thus, Paton conflates at least two events—a process at work throughout the social-historical events described in the novel. One of the other shanty towns was called Tobruk, which is mentioned specifically by Paton in connexion which Michael Scott in *Apartheid and the Archbishop,* 153.

forced to live.[30] Arthur Jarvis left a paper on Native[31] crime half-written at the time of his murder, directed at the consciences of the white population of South Africa. The irony of his murder is thus sharpened and deepened.

The foregoing analysis illustrates the use Paton makes throughout the novel of actual social events. They are not there simply for their own sakes, as important as they are. They do not simply add background or convincingness to the whole by making sociological 'facts' concrete (although they do this in passing). They are tied to particular fictional events, characters and consequences. They work functionally.

First, Stephen Kumalo leaves the remote Natal village of Ndotsheni and travels hundreds of miles in a train to the thoroughly (for him) alien and bewildering city of Johannesburg. He searches for days amongst the soulless townships for his son, scurrying from Sophiatown to Alexandra, to Claremont, to Pimville, to Orlando, back and forth, unsuccessful, tormented, tired and depressed. It is during this fruitless endless searching that he encounters the Alexandra Bus Boycott, as we have seen. The boycott is a kind of analogue of his own emotional and physical journeying that is getting him nowhere. It is a suitable metaphor of frustration for both Stephen Kumalo, the fictional individual, and the actual African workers. It is a crisis point for Kumalo: he begins to suspect and fear the truth about his son. Later, he confirms this:

> —At first it was a search. I was anxious at first, but as the search went on, step by step, so did the anxiety turn to fear, and

---

[30] See series of articles by Paton on the relation between society and the offender in *The Forum*, quoted in Callan, *Alan Paton*, 145-6; and Paton's *Tales From a Troubled Land* (New York, Charles Scribner, 1961: published in London in the same year by Jonathan Cape as *Debbie Go Home*), *passim*.

[31] 'Native' was the term used in Government papers, in official documents, in newspapers and in ordinary parlance at that time. Post-Verwoerd, it became 'Bantu' [sic]. Thereafter the South African Broadcasting Company, which was Government controlled, began to use the term 'African' and to refer to particular Africans by name in news bulletins. Paton himself never used 'native'. It is employed here for obvious reasons.

> this fear grew deeper step by step. It was at Alexandra that I first grew afraid, but it was here in your House, when we heard of the murder, that my fear grew into something too great to be borne.[32]

By causing Kumalo to encounter the Bus Boycott, Paton associates a private and personal trauma with a social one, linking an imagined and a real crisis. Later, ironically, Absalom is able to hide himself among the walkers; it helps Absalom and hinders his father, another significant linking. While Absalom mingles with the boycotters, his father, at the Mission for the Blind, at Ezenzeleni, suddenly has his eyes opened to the truth about his son. Thus, the entire incident is made to work on more than one level.

Second, Shanty Town: its relation to the murder we have already examined. Its function in relation to Stephen Kumalo is twofold: it helps to convince the general reader of the dispiriting extent of Kumalo's search, and to impress the South African reader with the extent of social injustice in his own land. Further it makes another 'step' in the search Kumalo describes in the extract just quoted.

Chapter VIII ends with Msimangu and Stephen Kumalo returning to Sophiatown from Alexandra. The main story-line (of their search) continues at the beginning of Chapter IX:

> While Kumalo was waiting for Msimangu to take him to Shanty Town, he spent the time with Gertrude and her child.[33]

As far as the main narrative of the quest is concerned, the story could have been taken up from this point, without Kumalo having to be shown in Shanty Town. But the need for psychological convincingness means that we must watch Kumalo's fear growing throughout his search in Shanty Town. We are thus persuaded of Shanty Town's

---

[32] *Cry, the Beloved Country*, Bk I, ch. xv, 94.

[33] Ibid., Bk. I, ch. x, 55.

fictional reality, besides knowing that it is also a historical reality. Not only that; immediately after his sojourn in there, Kumalo returns to the Mission only to discover that, while he has been searching for his son, Absalom committed murder at 1.30 p.m. on that very day, and his fear 'grew into something too great to be borne'. The social and the personal have become aspects of a single reality: the fictional event has been encapsulated in the social event, the outward becoming the mirror and the metaphor of the inner.

What then, does Paton achieve by altering historical events to occur either later or earlier, and by putting the events themselves out of historical sequence? The answer seems to be that his artistic purpose necessitates the reader in grasping the point that personal tragedy (especially of the Africans) and social evils are inextricably linked. Such an interpretation of social events obviously implies a certain kind of programme to remedy such social evils. In other words, one infers a positive political stance in the writer which, he hopes, will bring about a change in his readers' political and social attitudes. And, as Paton's historical 'distortions' clearly show, political attitudes and social tragedies are human ones first.

Paton's 'plain and simple truth' of the 'social record', then, is neither as simple or plain as he claims. Nor, indeed, is his 'truth' quite as obvious as he implies. The plainness and simplicity of his 'truth' depends very much on the placing of a specific interpretation on the political and social events concerned, and on seeing their relationship to personal dilemmas in a particular way. Many will accept his 'truth' as axiomatic; many will not. It is clear, too, that in the South Africa of 1947, when Paton wrote the book, he himself believed that his plain and simple truth was far from obvious. For who would bother to write a novel to persuade people of the obvious? The 'Author's Note' was just the first shot in his arsenal of persuasive rhetoric, which is the novel itself.

About Roy Holland

Roy Holland was born in Birmingham. He went to Africa in 1966 to teach in the universities of the Boleswa countries. In 1971 he went to Greece for three years. He and his family lived on the island of Levkas for six months, the Gulf of Corinth for a similar period, and in Corfu for a little over two years. He wrote full-time until 1974, when he returned to the U.K. and worked on a research project until returning to Africa in 1977. Thereafter he lived in Southern Africa and worked in universities in Zimbabwe, Lebowa and Venda. He was Professor of English at the University of the North, the University of Venda, as well as Dean of the Faculty of Arts in the later 80's. He retired early to write full-time, and now lives in Ledbury, Herefordshire.

www.ingramcontent.com/pod-product-compliance
Ingram Content Group UK Ltd.
Pitfield, Milton Keynes, MK11 3LW, UK
UKHW041435180426
11947UKWH00007B/458